With Complie

Foreword

Life is a journey into the unknown. Sometimes it excites us and at other times throws challenges at us. What I have made of this journey is what I have attempted to describe in this book. I do not claim to have achieved any great deed or having excelled in any particular field. This is not an autobiography but my humble attempt at describing my life as I have experienced it and lived it.

A key turning point in my life was the re-igniting of my interest in yoga. Following a teaching diploma from British Wheel of Yoga and a few years of teaching, I started concentrating on my personal practice at home. My focus gradually shifted to holistic aspects of yoga, which helped me develop a complete practice and publish a book "Develop Health and Inner Peace Through Meditational Yoga".

My practice of yoga has not only helped me maintain good health but it has also made me more spiritual and at peace with myself. For the past few years, I have adopted a morning routine of an hour and half of yoga, a cup of tea while watching the news, a refreshing shower, daily prayer (*samayak paath*) and a healthy breakfast. This four-hour routine sets me up nicely for the day with enthusiasm and a positive outlook.

The book is not in a chronological order as I found it impossible to do the same. However, I trust the readers would find some logic and order in this sequence of madness.

The theme behind our holidays has been, "The love of our family and friends is the greatest blessing in life." I strongly advocate it and have covered it in the book in the chapter 'Lifetime of Holidays'.

I thank God for what I have been granted in life, which is more than what I deserve or what I could have possibly asked for

"Believe in yourself, have a positive outlook in life, live life with passion and conviction and you will find most things would fall into place."

Peace
Jiwan D Jain

Content List

Sr. No.	Content	Page

1. Formative Years

As I am writing about some memorable incidents from my life, why not start from the time of my birth, which is 10 November 1945.

My father was a devout Jain who followed the religion with utmost dedication and discipline and observed all the tenets of Jainism. He visited the temple everyday where he would perform his daily *pooja* (prayer) in proper Digambar tradition and spend a couple of hours there. At the time of my birth, my father was in his pooja and was informed of my birth after finishing the same. He was obviously delighted with the occasion and on reaching home announced that I will be named Jiwandhar, after the *muni* (sage) whose pooja he had just performed that day.

Being an officer for the Government of India, my father was entitled to government accommodation. His inclination towards the Jain religion made him opt for a house on Raja Bazar Road, which had a Jain temple at one end, literally a stone's throw from our house. It was in fact a sought-after area for Jains with most of the properties being occupied by Jain families. Ours was a terraced house with two bedrooms, a lounge, a kitchen, a storeroom, a bathroom, a small courtyard at the back and a little veranda in the front. The front of the house also had a small path and a green hedge that shielded the view of the house from the main road. The lane at the back of our house led to a small centre known as Nishya-ji where a lot of community and cultural activities took place.

Most residents on Raja Bazar Road worked for the central government, had jobs at similar levels and were of nearly the same age, which meant that they also had children of similar age groups. The children could perhaps be best described as falling into three bands, little ones like us who bonded well with the boys and girls playing together; a group which was a few years older to us (perhaps 10 to 16) who had a separate group for boys doing their sporting activities and a girls group where you would always hear giggles and laughter; and the third group of the older sisters and brothers who indulged in activities suited to their age group.

With a very close community spirit, all neighbourhood elders were addressed as uncles and aunties. It is worth describing some of the key families that I remember. We occupied house number 41 and in house number 42 lived Mr Hans Kumar Jain who had a taste for fine things in life. He owned a car, I think an old Austin, and the family also owned a refrigerator. Both these things were a rare possession in those days. Once in a blue moon we would get a ride in the car, which was a big treat for us. Uncle Jugmander Das Jain lived in house number 48 and had his younger brother and his wife (Trishla aunty) sharing the house with him. Both Trishla aunty and my mother belonged to Uttar Pradesh (UP) and became very good friends. Another family I would like to mention here is of suave and sophisticated Mittal uncle who lived in house number 31. He had two very beautiful daughters, Parul who was my elder sister's age and Shameem who was my age. More about her later!

I was quite a bold and witty child, always trying to make people laugh. My mother, who we addressed as *bhabho,* often used a colloquial phrase from UP '*yun kahiyo*'. And sometimes when bhabho would ask me to go and give a message to Trishla aunty, I would go there and say, "Bhabho has said '*yun kahiyo*'...... followed by the message." Trishla aunty would burst out laughing hearing this.

India gained independence in 1947, a couple of years after my birth, and this was followed by partition at its tail. This was a very disturbing period with violence on the streets and a lot of fear amongst all the communities. I remember our fathers equipping themselves with large wooden batons and other protective equipment and standing guard at night at the ends of the street. Fortunately, the community came out of this unscathed and normal life could resume.

CELEBRATING THE FESTIVALS

The whole community celebrated the festivals of Holi, Diwali *and raksha-bandhan* amongst others. There was a buzz and excitement in the air from a few days before the festivals with all the preparations and plans being put in place. Diwali in particular was a huge event as there was a competitive spirit in who will make the best *kandeel* (Chinese lanterns) and whose fireworks will have the best display. Yes, we used to make some of our own fireworks – fountain in particular, for which we would go hunting for materials like iron filings, cobalt, copper sulphate crystals, etc. Everyone made their decorative kandeels and hung them above the hedge in the front of their house. On the day of Diwali the road was lit up with all these decorative lanterns and the community decided whose display and fireworks were the best.

Diwali was followed by *bhaiya-dooj* to celebrate the special bond between brothers and sisters. It was very much a family affair, but was still celebrated with much excitement and joy with plenty of food and sweets on offer.

Preparations for the celebration of Holi started much in advance. Our mothers made the sweets. Particular favourites for the occasion were *gujiya, shakkar pare, khoya peda, besan laddoo* and others. We had a special task of collecting lots of *har-singar* flowers, remove their petals and dry their stems. These were then ground into paste and used to make the saffron coloured water for Holi. On the actual day, all members of the family came out in the neighbourhood and applied *gulal* (fine powder in various colours) on each other and offered sweets. After this, the men folk formed a group and stood at one end of the road with gulal and sweets. They welcomed everyone who came there and then handed them over to us kids. Depending on the age of the person, we either just threw some coloured water on them or gave them a full dip in the tub of water prepared with the paste of har-singar flowers. The memory of celebrating these festivals with the whole neighbourhood brings real joy and happiness even today.

There were also a number of other religious festivals for which the whole community came together in organising and taking part. Key one of these was Mahavir Jayanti, the celebration of the birth of lord Mahavir. Many a times a statue of lord Mahavir was placed on a high seat in a horse drawn chariot which was taken around the area with all the followers dressed in festive clothes singing Jain hymns and *bhajans*. To keep the lord's statue steady, one person was seated behind it in the chariot. This person was chosen from the community based on the highest bid made as donation to the temple and my father would often contest for this and win. I and/or my brother would have the honour to sit in the front of the chariot along with the charioteer when my father would win the bid.

Another festival that had much of a religious fervour to it was the *Das-lakshan Parva*, a ten days celebration that ended with *Shamavani*. This was a time for individuals to introspect and attempt to correct their ways. Shamavani means forgiving others and asking for their forgiveness for anything you may have done to cause them hurt by your thoughts, words or deeds. The word Das-lakshan can be defined as ten (*das*) characteristics (*lakshan*) of the Jain religion, which define the very essence of Jainism and I came to learn about these at a much later age. All these characteristics are preceded by the word *uttam,* which means supreme.

- *uttam kshama* – forgiveness (forgive others and seek their forgiveness)
- *uttam mardav* – humility in thinking (lack of feeling of ego, lowliness and worthlessness)
- *uttam arjav* – straight forwardness (honesty, purity in behaviour)
- *uttam satya* – truthfulness in words and actions
- *uttam shauch* – purity, cleanliness of soul, which can otherwise be contaminated by our deeds
- *uttam sanyam* – self-restraint, control over our senses (*indriyan*)
- *uttam tapa* – austerity, control of our urges and desires
- *uttam tyag* – renunciation, charity
- *uttam akinchaya – aparigrah* – non-possessiveness (not acquiring more than necessary for our use)
- *uttam brhamcharya* – celibacy (control over sensual tendencies)

The festival of Das-lakshan Parva is celebrated by doing a daily pooja and reading the scriptures in the temple, focussing on one of these principles on consecutive days.

Comprehending the above invigorated my faith in the religion and this is when I truly became a Jain. I understood the very scientific basis of Jainism and how relevant it is in the world today than it has ever been. Jainism does not have a concept of God as the almighty with some extraordinary powers, instead there are twenty four *Tirthankaras*. These are considered to be someone like us but who attained nirvana or salvation by following the above principles and going into Samadhi (deep meditation). There is an inherent understanding in Jainism that we are all capable of achieving nirvana like them by following this path.

I have given these here not in furtherance of the religion but because of my belief that if people around the world were to follow these principles in their life, we may not all achieve nirvana, but there would certainly be much peace and less conflict in the world.

Another religious activity that my father was involved in was reading of scriptures and explaining their meaning to the audience. This would be a weekly activity for a few months of the year and it gave my father a nickname *bhagat-ji* meaning a pious person.

We belong to the community of Digambar Jains in which the *sadhus* (monks) follow the tradition of collecting alms for their daily meal from the households of the followers of the religion. The sadhus observe a strict discipline according to which they decide in the morning on what they will accept as alms on a particular day and if it is not offered, they go without a meal. We had one occasion when a group of sadhus were due to come to our street. Everyone got together and decided on alms that each household would prepare and stand outside their house to offer it. The sadhus arrived on the assigned day and started walking past the alms on offer. Someone observed that they hesitated in front of one of the houses but then decided to walk on. The message was sent across that it may be the right alms but one of the conditions may not have been right. Probably the couple was not standing and offering the alms together. We had also prepared the same alms. Thus, when the sadhus came, my mum and dad stood together and offered the meal to them. There was a great feeling of jubilation in the whole community when the offer was accepted at our house. All the ladies from the neighbourhood came together to help as well as observe the ceremony and receive the blessings from the sadhus.

Another thing we looked forward to with excitement were our summer holidays. All the children of our age group would wake up early in the morning and head towards the Shivaji Park (formerly called Hockey Ground) situated near the Jain temple. We played several games to keep us occupied for 2 to 3 hours and thoroughly enjoy ourselves. Most of these games were simple and provided a lot of action, fun, joviality and bonding.

I still remember some of the games we played:

- *langdi-taang* (one person hops on one leg and tries to catch the other players running inside a marked area)
- *kho-kho* (usually played in teams where the players of one team sit on their haunches in a line, with alternate players facing in the opposite direction. One player who is the catcher tries to catch the target player from the

other team who runs around the line of sitting players - the catcher can touch the back of any sitting player who then takes over the task of catching)
- *kanche* (a game played with marbles)
- *piththoo* (a player of one team takes a ball and hits a tower made of 9-10 stones from a marked line and his team has to re-assemble the stones before the other team gets the ball back and hits them with it)
- *rassa* (two players hold a rope from both ends and swing it while another player jumps over it)
- *gulli-danda* (two competing teams try to get the *gulli* which is a small barrel-shaped wooden object to reach the finish line first by flicking it up in the air and then hitting it with a stick called *danda*, repeating the process till the line is crossed)
- *staapu* (hopscotch)
- variety of card games
- hide and seek

and many more.

The variety of games helped develop strength, stamina, speed, balance and coordination. Even at this young age the group activities would help develop soft skills of team working, leadership/ taking ownership, and sportsmanship (meaning it is as important to take part as it is to win).

After the morning session, we would go home, have our bath and breakfast, and then assemble again for some more activities. These would vary and include some more games, picking fruits from the garden of one of the neighbour's courtyard or visiting Nishya-ji to take part in some activities. At lunch time, we would all just land up at one of the houses where aunty would take care of our meal. Our mums were sure that if we didn't turn up at home for lunch, we must be well taken care of wherever we were.

One of the other attractions of our summer vacation was the exchange visits to our maternal uncle's house. Our cousins would come to stay with us for a few days and we would go to theirs afterwards. They lived in Daryaganj in old Delhi and a popular attraction for us was the hawkers who would come selling Indian street food like *chaat-pakori* (Indian savoury) and *kulfi* (Indian ice cream). My uncle loved to see us enjoying ourselves and would ask these hawkers to sit in the courtyard of the house and not leave until everyone had their fill.

It was rather fortunate that we had a boy's school just across the road from our house. It was a Bengali school but as the medium of education was Hindi and English it suited me just fine. One big advantage of being close to the school was that I could just run up to the school when the bell rang in the morning. Our school had an assembly every morning and a bell would be rung to signal everyone to get in their place. This gave me enough time to run from home and take my place in the line.

I was a bright student in school. However, with a stroke of bad luck, I fell ill just before the final exams of class 8, which were to determine our choice of subjects for Higher Secondary. My results were not good enough for me to opt for the science stream. My father was particularly disappointed as he wanted me to pursue a career in Engineering, which would require me to qualify with science subjects. He went to meet the Principal to discuss if something could be done. The Principal was very understanding knowing my previous academic record but found himself unable to do anything to change my stream. As I was one of the youngest students in class, my father proposed to him to permit me to repeat the year and if I did well, he could then allow me to get the subjects of my choice. The Principal agreed to this and was pleased with his decision, as I became the school topper in the higher secondary exams three years later.

With my father's quick promotions, we moved to a bigger house on Irwin Road and within a couple of years, to a bungalow in Bangla Sahib Lane. Being opposite the Bangla Sahib Gurdwara, the bungalows on the lane were occupied mostly by Sikh families. Ours being the corner bungalow, we had a decent size garden on the side which was developed as a badminton court by my father where all the children came and played in the summer holidays. There was also a vacant plot of land at the back of our house, which we converted, into a vegetable garden.

Here too, the atmosphere was very friendly with a good community spirit amongst the neighbours who were also quite well placed in government jobs. Mr Giani was a Personal Assistant to a minister, Mr Bhalla was a Personal Secretary to the Food and Agriculture minister and there was a Bengali neighbour who was the Deputy Auditor General. Mr Giani was a very pious person and used to read the 'Guru Granth Saheb' at the Gurdwara. However, his children were not inclined in the same way. So, whenever he would ask his sons to visit the Gurdwara, they would reluctantly agree and ask me to accompany them. The incentive offered was that there would be a lot of very good-looking Punjabi girls visiting the Gurdwara to which I could not say no.

The location of our house was brilliant and offered us a lot of opportunities. There was a YMCA on one side of our house where I used to go for roller-skating. Connaught place was a mere 5 minutes walk with all the picture halls, eating-places and shopping.

My father worked at the All India Radio (AIR) building on Parliament Street, just a 10 minute walk from our house. I still remember it being a beautiful round structure with a colonnade type veranda on its periphery. Often when we visited my father, we would sneak a run around the building in this veranda and have a lot of fun. The seat of government, namely the Houses of Parliament, was at the end of Parliament Street that was also within a walking distance from our house.

The area around the Houses of Parliament has splendour of its own, with Rashtrapati Bhavan (residence of the President of India) sitting majestically at the top of Raisina Hill, flanked on the right and left by two secretariat buildings called North and South Block. Coming down Raisina hill, the road called Rajpath leads straight down to India Gate, the war memorial of the martyrs of the First World War. Rajpath is a tree-lined avenue with a man-made lake behind sets of trees on both sides. During summer, a boating club is set up in the lake for public use.

Rajpath was our haunt during the summer holidays. We would go there for a jog or to pick fruits (mulberry and *gatte*) from the trees lining the road or to do boating. Grounds around the lake also provided room for other games and activities. I remember a small incident when one summer as we were picking the fruits, a man came running to us and said that we could not pick the fruits since he had taken the contract for them now. However, this did not stop us as the road was very long and one man could not possibly oversee all of us.

REPUBLIC DAY PARADE

This event from the school days has left a rather sweet memory in my mind. I had an opportunity to take part in that year's Republic Day Parade on 26th January. A group of Scouts/NCC Cadets were selected from across the schools in Delhi and I was one of the lucky ones amongst them. After a number of days of preparations we marched past in the contingent from the Houses of Parliament, along Rajpath, past the President's enclosure to finish at Patiala House where we were served refreshments. When I think back it does not seem such a great deal but at that time we felt so excited and proud to be a part of this national celebration.

Although I passed higher secondary with first division with a distinction in Maths, the percentage was not good enough for me to get admission in the engineering college in Delhi. As my parents did not agree to send me to another city, I decided to take admission in Ramjas College to study B.Sc. Physics Honours. Classes for some subjects like English and Maths were held at the college but the classes for Science subjects for honours students of all colleges were held jointly at the Delhi University campus. These classes had both boys and girls, which was obviously a new experience for me. One day, while going with a group of friends for a class at the University, I came face to face with Shameem who was also with her friends. We had met each other after a good ten years and what a beauty she had turned out to be! She stopped to talk to me and we had a long chat while our friends waited a distance away. I think she did much of the talking between us. When I joined my friends, they pulled my leg with various remarks, "You didn't tell us that you know her; She is supposed to be one of the beauty queens of the University; How about introducing us to her!" and so on.

―✳―

2. IIT college days

INDIAN INSTITUTE OF TECHNOLOGY (IIT)

By a stroke of luck, Delhi College of Engineering in Hauz Khas became an IIT while I was still in the first year at Delhi University. I applied for the national Joint Entrance Examination (JEE), got selected and joined the B. Tech, Electrical Engineering course. It was compulsory for all students at IIT Delhi to stay in the hostels. In the first year we had to share a room with another classmate, which worked well as it eased the separation from home. In the following years, we were to move to our own independent rooms. In the first year I was allocated a room in Vindhyachal House with S P Jain as my partner.

Ragging was a part and parcel of hostel life in colleges those days, and IIT was no different. Given a choice, the freshers would have liked to disappear in thin air for the first few days to avoid being picked for it. Very soon we became aware of the names of the worst ragging groups and the key names that filled the list were Vora, Ahuja and Binder.

It was perhaps the third or the fourth day of college when I happened to notice someone standing in the queue at our mess at lunchtime. I walked up to him and tapped him on the shoulder saying, "Borker is that you?" He turned around and asked, "Hello Jiwan, how are you? Have you just joined this year as I have not seen you before?" After a brief chat, he told me to just mention his name if there was any problem (referring indirectly to ragging).

Unfortunately my partner and I got picked by two of the students of Vora's group and were taken to his room. He asked us 'where we came from', 'what school did we attend', 'what stream were we in' and after this introduction he asked 'if we knew anyone at IIT Delhi'. I told him that I knew Suresh Borker who was a close friend of mine at school. Surprisingly his tone changed completely and he asked how we were settling down in the hostel and that if there were any problems we should contact him. He told us that we could go back to our rooms. This totally baffled us and the mystery was solved when we discovered later that Suresh was the topper at IIT and was highly respected in the college and not only that Vora was in Electrical Engineering stream as was Suresh.

The time spent at IIT was perhaps the best period of my life as we made a lot of friends and learned to live our life independently. The hostels at IITD were very well organized and the mess offered a wide variety of healthy food that was varied and delicious. Thursdays were assigned for western meals. We used to still go home on the weekends, initially every week but with time this tailed off to a lesser frequency.

There is no doubt that students came to IIT with a serious focus on studies in order to develop a good career and life for themselves. However, boys won't be boys if they did not do some mischief and play pranks. I still remember some interesting incidents of my IIT days, which I would like to share here.

At the time when we were in IIT, there were only two hostels with an undeveloped area next to them. It was very much like a forest. One of the ragging groups picked up a fresher with his cot and gently left him in this area to play a prank on him. He was aghast when he woke up and everyone had a good laugh when he came back with his cot and bedding.

During summer months we used to pull our cots out in the veranda in front of our rooms to sleep in the fresh air at night. One of our colleagues was a very sound sleeper. One night while he was fast asleep, we picked up his cot and placed it under the shower in the bathroom. One boy even cut the string holding his pyjamas and turned the shower on as we all ran out. Rest can be imagined!

Many students of the hostel had bikes to go around the campus. They chained their bikes to the railings at the bottom of the staircase in the hostel. One of the early skills we had learned as an engineer was to pick bicycle locks. If three or four of us wanted to go for a movie late in the evening, we would pick the locks of couple of bikes, go to the local cinema in Yusuf Sarai and place the bikes back in their place on return.

In the third year, I was moved to a new hostel named Aravali where I was allocated a room at the end of the corridor on the third floor. There was a balcony in front of my room and Ram Mohan occupied the room next to the balcony. Next to my room were D Koley and then S Sood. Although all three of them were in Mechanical Engineering, four of us got along very well together.

One evening, when I came back from dinner, I found my room locked from inside. I soon discovered that someone had pulled the upper bolt of the door from inside and then shut the window above it. Fortunately, the window had a wire-mesh in the middle, which I was able to break and get my hand in to open the bolt to get in. I found out the person responsible for this and decided to return the favour. One evening, when Ram Mohan had gone for dinner, I locked his door by closing the lower bolt of the door. When he came back, he realized that there was no way he could get in without breaking the door down. But he showed real guts and decided to go through his room's open window by climbing on the railings of the balcony – a daring task but it worked. Scores settled, we all got together and decided to play the prank on the entire hostel by locking all the bathroom doors from inside. To provide an escape route, we left the bathrooms on one floor undisturbed. The chaos this caused next morning was quite something, till the time the warden got a handyman to break the window grills and unlock the bathrooms.

One day, a friend of ours lost his room keys and got locked out of his room. We all tried our keys and managed to open the door with one of them. One day four of us had gone to get water from the water cooler in the mess. In jest, we tried our key in the door of the storeroom and it opened. We decided to take some items like bread, butter, eggs, sugar and flour from it. One of our colleagues was a keen cook and brought a gas stove from home to cook for us. After this, we would have a feast of *parathas*, omelettes or *halwa* in the room whenever it took our fancy.

One of the extra-curricular activities I got interested in was astronomy. I joined the Astronomy Club and undertook a project of making a reflective telescope with Ravi as my partner. We were having difficulty in finding a piece of glass of the size and quality we needed to make the telescope. Fortunately, a friend of my father who owned

Jayna Watch Company managed to obtain one for us from Switzerland. When complete, this glass would have given us the largest reflective telescope in India. Ravi and I spent hours grinding the surface of the glass to the curvature we required. We had reached the final stage of glass to glass grinding and polishing when a hasty action by one of the laboratory staff produced a crack in the middle of the glass. Sadly, we just could not find another similar piece of and had to abandon the project.

One of my best friends at IIT was Ravinder Mathur. He was the one and only person in our group who had got a distinction in English in Higher Secondary examinations. I often wondered what was it that gave him that unique honour? Working closely with him, I realized that he had an art of using just the right words and put them together so clearly and precisely that he could describe something in one sentence that most people may need a whole paragraph to describe.

I was given the nickname 'Jammu' in IIT (no idea how this came about or what, if any, association it had with my name). But Ravi always preferred to call me James, as if he had some premonition of me emigrating to Britain sometime in the future. He lived in Bengali Market, which was towards the other end of Connaught Place from where I lived in Bangla Sahib Lane. During summer holidays or if we were visiting home on the weekend, I would walk up to Bengali Market to meet Ravi and we would have the famous *chaat* or *gol-guppas* there. At other times we would meet in Connaught Place and after a walk around the circle, we would go for a cup of coffee to Standard Coffee House, which was famous for its coffee and cookies that accompanied it.

Connaught Place, abbreviated to CP, is a famous place in Delhi consisting of a large circular park encircled with two concentric rings of two storey buildings in Georgian architecture with a colonnade in front. The buildings house several shops, commercial offices, restaurants and places of entertainment. These rings of buildings, known as inner and outer circle, are broken into blocks by seven roads radiating from the central park. Painted in white, the glorious architecture of CP gives it a regal look making it a major tourist attraction.

Ravi and I were partners in crime in many adventures and also in the final graduation project in which we designed and developed a ten-digit digital counter. Soon after graduating, I got a job in a firm in Madras. I moved there and stayed with my uncle's family. I held this job for about 8 months and then moved back to Delhi to take up a job in Food Storage Electrical Circle. This is when I encountered first hand the systemic corruption in the government. As I took the responsibility of my role as an assistant engineer, the previous officer started explaining to me about the area that he covered and the contractors who were working in that area. He also started briefing me about the commission arrangements with the contractors. When I told him that I was not interested in that aspect, he kept quiet. Later during lunch, another officer told me secretly that even if I was not interested in working with the commission arrangement, I should not stop it otherwise it will spoil matters for whoever comes after me. In fact, he suggested that I may pass it to another officer in the team.

Some years later, I came to UK and Ravi joined Bhabha Atomic Research Centre (BARC). He and I stayed in touch and would always meet whenever I visited India. Later, he also came on a visit to London and we went to a hotel on the banks of river Thames. While we were having a quiet drink in the restaurant, there was a bit of commotion and we noticed that people were moving towards the windows. As we turned our heads around, we were amazed to see that the Tower Bridge was lifting up to allow a tall ship to pass through. It was surprising and quite a coincidence that having lived in London for over twenty years I had never seen the bridge opening up before this.

3. Family life

MARRIAGE TO VEENA

November 1969 was a turning point when I got married to my life partner Veena. She came across as a shy girl initially but over time I began to discover her wonderful qualities and started appreciating them and still do. She has a beautiful smile, an infectious laughter and superb cooking skills, which are unparalleled in our circle of friends. She is also a terrific homemaker and a wonderful mother to our two lovely children. Despite all the ups and downs we faced in our life, I would not wish to trade my life and the time we have spent together for anything.

At the time of my marriage, I was working for Food Storage Electrical Circle that had its office in the residential area of Jorbagh. One day I made a plan to go to meet my elder sister who lived just a few miles away in Lakshmi Nagar. The same morning, Vinod dropped in to see me and after introducing him to my colleagues, I also happened to mention that I was planning to go to my sister for lunch. One of my colleagues insisted that I take his motorcycle as we may have to wait for a long time for a bus during office hours. While we were going along the main road, we met with an accident when an army officer's car suddenly turned in front of our bike and threw us both off. There was not much damage to the bike but I bruised my knee and injured my chin. The army officer took us immediately to the military hospital where we were attended to and discharged. We thanked him and reached my sister's house. She was initially shocked to see me in that condition but was soon relieved that there was nothing serious. While explaining the incident to her, I said pointing to Vinod, "Look what kind of a friend I have got! First, I get thrown off the bike and while I am lying wounded on the road, he decides to throw himself on top of me." We all laughed at my comment and the atmosphere became lighter. My sister lovingly served us lunch followed by turmeric milk, which she insisted we both must have to help our wounds heal faster. Back at work, my friend whose bike we had taken, brushed off the damage to the bike saying I don't need to worry about it and he'll get that fixed himself. I feel very fortunate to be surrounded by such caring people in my life.

I was perhaps the second person in our electrical batch to get married. One of my close friends Lalit Nayar said that he would not be able to attend my marriage as he was leaving for UK and would not be in Delhi on the day of my wedding. In further discussion with him, I came to know that UK was readily offering visas to engineering graduates from IIT Delhi. When I discussed the subject with Veena, she was absolutely thrilled with the prospect and I immediately applied for a visa. I left for UK in April and Veena was to join me four months later in August.

ARRIVAL IN THE U.K.

Lalit Nayar had decided to pick me up in London and we agreed to meet at Victoria Station at 6 pm. I came out of Heathrow Airport and headed straight to the information desk to enquire about how to go to the Victoria Station. I was directed to a coach stand just outside the airport from where a coach took me straight there. As my flight had arrived quite early, I managed to get some food and waited at the Victoria Coach Station for Lalit. I waited till about 20 minutes past 6 and there was no sign of him. Those were the days with no mobile phones and I had no way of getting in touch with him. Suddenly it stuck me if there was another Victoria Station? I was informed that there was a train station by the same name about a quarter of a mile down the road. I started walking towards it with my luggage trolley. Lalit applied the same logic and having gone to the train station was told about the Victoria Coach Station where I had been waiting. We met each other half way between the two stations and heaved a sigh of relief. I stayed with him for a couple of days until I found a place to rent near him in Clapham Junction.

The same evening, I made my first visit to a pub where we met a number of other IITians who were already in London. One of our friends Bhatti, who was working at Plessey, said his company was recruiting people and suggested I go with him the next day to his office. I met his supervisor who explained that Plessey manufactured RF Transmitter/Receivers for the military and he was responsible for their testing and quality assurance. He gave me a test script and asked me to carry out the test of one of the units and complete the test report. At the end of the test, he offered me a job as a tester with an hourly stipend of 10s 9p. He asked me if I would be interested and when I could start. In my anxiety, I said I could start the next day. Gauging my excitement, he smiled and said, "Tomorrow is Friday. You could perhaps start from Monday instead". And that is how my first job began in London. Soon I made two good friends at Plessey, one Nasib Bansal who offered me a room on rent at his house and another Balraj Jain about whom I'll talk about later.

As my key objective of coming to London was to gain experience in the field of computers and then go back to

India, I had therefore applied for a job to a couple of Information Technology (IT) firms too. After a written test and a few interviews, I got a job as Systems Engineer with International Computers Limited (ICL) and I joined them soon after.

One of my close friends from IIT Satish Aggarwal introduced me to Vijay Gupta one of his neighbourhood friends from India. Vijay had just come back from India after getting married and was waiting for his wife to come and join him. In the meanwhile, Veena also arrived here in August and we were invited to their place for our first meal. And we have become the best of friends ever since.

Maneesh's arrival:

Veena was expecting our first child when she came to London. Maneesh was born on 28 November 1970 at St Thomas Hospital, just across the river Thames from the Houses of Parliament. In those days they would keep the mother and child in the hospital for 5-6 days as a part of postnatal care. Thus, they would both wake up in the morning to the chimes and sight of the Big Ben from their bedside window. What a welcome to London for Maneesh!

The day we brought Maneesh home from the hospital, it was a cold, freezing, snowy morning with visibility down to a few yards. We were both excited with this new chapter in our life and spend as much time with him as we could. Maneesh was a delightful child, a bundle of fun and joy. He will have his feed regularly and be happy and content throughout the day. In summer we found every opportunity to take him out for sightseeing, picnic or socialising with friends.

Unfortunately, the apartment we had rented had a bit of dampness due to which Veena became severely asthmatic. With Maneesh in a very delicate stage, we felt deeply concerned about him catching the same. The prospect of sending him to India was heart breaking for both of us but on the other hand the risk of him catching the disease was equally disturbing. After a discussion with the family back home, we took the decision to send him to India to temporarily stay with my parents. On one side we were both feeling very sad at the thought of parting with him at this early stage of his life but on the other hand we were comforted in the knowledge that he will be loved by all the members of the family and will be taken good care of. We immediately started working on buying our own place and moved in our house in late 1972. Following year we brought Maneesh back to us from India and held a coming home party for him. From then on we spent a lot of time with him to make up for the lost moments.

Purchase of first car:

As my work required me to travel around quite a lot, I felt the need to buy a car. I took driving lessons and was fortunate to get the licence in the first attempt. I had just about enough money in the bank to get myself a second-hand car and decided to purchase a Vauxhall Viva. The seller lived in Theydon Bois in Essex, which was quite a distance from my apartment in Clapham Common. Although she was kind enough to bring the car to my place of work for me to examine it but I had to go and collect it from her home address after finalizing the deal. It was not the most pleasant journey for me back home being a novice driver, driving a new car, and having no knowledge of the area. I purchased the London A to Z and chalked out the route but had to still stop a number of times on the way to double check. Finally, I reached home heaving a sigh of relief.

The car gave us greater opportunities to explore London. We made the best use of our newfound freedom to travel. We started socialising and going out on journeys and visits on the weekends. We became carefree and let our fancy take us wherever.

Camping holiday to Europe:

Gradually our circle of friends expanded and we started enjoying life, going out as often as we could. We also became good friends with another young couple and started planning a holiday to the European continent. With our meagre resources, we decided to go on a camping trip covering Holland, France, Germany, Austria and Switzerland. Planning the holidays was in itself a lot of fun - we would get together on the weekend and sit down with a couple of beers and plan the holiday in great detail chalking out the countries and cities to visit, identifying suitable camping sites and booking them for the precise dates when we would be there. I acquired the street maps of major cities we were going to stay at and our friend Santosh started learning German, which would be helpful in Germany and other places where it was well understood. There was tremendous excitement but also a bit of apprehension, as I did not have the driving experience for such a long journey or the experience of driving on the other side of the road. Finally, we went for the trip as planned.

It turned out to be one of the most memorable and enjoyable experiences of our life. We covered a large number of cities including Amsterdam, Frankfurt, Munich, Berne, Geneva, Innsbruck and Paris. Some of the camping sites we had chosen were remarkably good with all amenities and facilities.

Here I would like to share some memorable moments from the trip. Hope you will find them as interesting as I do.

One night, while we were asleep in the camping site in Amsterdam, it rained so much during the night that rainwater entered our tent and our beds got submerged in it. Amazing thing is that we didn't even feel it and kept sleeping. It was only when we got up in the morning did it dawn upon us that we were lying on a waterbed.

There was another interesting episode that took place in Frankfurt. While travelling, I asked Santosh to follow the map and guide me since I was driving. He asked me to give the name of the road we were on and I told him it was 'ein bahn strasse'. He searched for the name in the map but could not find it. He asked me to check again from the roadside. I saw another sign with the same name and repeated it to him. While he was still searching, I observed that the entire traffic was going only in one direction. Suddenly it dawned upon me that what I had been thinking of as a street name actually meant a one-way street: ein (one) and strasse (street). We all burst out laughing and poor chap could not hide his embarrassment that he was not able to spot the translation.

I also have particular memory of this beautiful site in Geneva where we pitched our tent just on the embankment of the river facing Lake Geneva with a clear view of the fountain in the middle of the lake. The site had very good facilities with a proper kitchen, a launderette and even some sports facilities. The ladies decided to make use of these and made stuffed *parathas* while we had a bottle of beer and a game of table tennis. The memories of the delicious hot *parathas* by the riverside are still fresh in my mind.

Not only did we have interesting incidents but some scary ones too. One such incident was when we were crossing from Austria to France and we had to go up the route through the Alps. As we were going uphill through the snow-laden road, the car started making weird sounds and behaving strangely. This made me realise my lack of driving experience particularly in snowy conditions. However, with some manoeuvring, we managed to pass through the area safely and reached Paris.

Finally, we returned home safe and sound with memories to last a lifetime.

Racial discrimination:

There was a phase in mid-seventies when Indians had to experience racial discrimination in the country. We had to face general abuse and foul language. Our ladies were easily identifiable due to the *bindi* they put on their forehead. Their handbags and jewellery were being snatched even in daylight and this phase came to be known as '*bindi* bashing'.

It was during these times that when I returned from work one day, Maneesh informed me that his Principal wanted to see me. I asked him if anything had happened in the school and he narrated the whole incident to me. He said that during lunch break, he was playing in the playground when 4-5 boys started bullying him and poking at him. In order to defend himself, he took out his belt and started whirling it around. The teacher in the playground saw him doing this and took him to the Principal.

I went to see his Principal the next day, who started by saying that what Maneesh did could not be tolerated in the school. I gently told him what had happened and also that if the same thing was to happen again, I would be quite happy to support Maneesh if he repeated the same action to defend himself. The Principal was a bit taken aback and said that he would not like any student to behave in this manner. However, he also said that he would make sure that the teachers keep the playground safe from any abuse of this type.

Becoming Self Dependent:

One day, my car developed a fault in its braking system. With the help of my engineer colleagues at work, I discovered that there was a leak in the brake cylinder. My colleagues were quite used to doing the servicing of their own vehicles and suggested that I could repair it myself. I decided to give it a try, bought the service manual for the car and managed to replace the faulty brake cylinder.

This incident made me realise the difference between the mindset of youth in India and here. Many of my friends from India who were qualified engineers never undertook any technical or maintenance work in the house, whereas the youngsters here, who were not even technically trained learnt to tackle most of these tasks themselves.

This incident also helped me develop a flair for DIY and I started managing the maintenance and repair jobs myself at home. Starting with simple jobs like painting and decorating, I ended up undertaking some major tasks like de-coking the engine of the car, re-spraying the whole car after the front wing got damaged in an accident and converting the two sitting rooms into a through-lounge by knocking down the partition wall. Both Veena and I enjoyed gardening and I also looked after our gardens at home with her.

I had developed a liking for good cars and bought myself a Volvo, which had a reputation for safety and reliability. I got an unfortunate incident to put this claim to test once. I had stopped at a traffic light when someone hit me with a bang from behind. The Volvo had solid steel bumpers in the front and at the back, which were further reinforced with a thick layer of solid rubber. As I came out of my car and saw the front of the car that had hit me, I was shocked to see its condition and dreaded the worse. But when I looked at the back of my car, there was no damage and even the bumper was totally intact. I was so relieved to see it that I did not put in a claim or report the accident, much to the delight of the driver of the car that had hit mine.

Sasha's Arrival:

To our utmost joy and celebration, Sasha arrived in our lives in 1977. We now had the pigeon pair and our family was complete. Sasha was a picture of beauty and we all just fell in love with her. Maneesh would hold her in his arms and enjoy the big brother feeling. We called her a little charmer as wherever we went; she would become the centre of attraction. Veena's elder sister who had come from India to be with her during her last days of pregnancy also doted over Sasha.

More Fun Trips:

I have always enjoyed driving and whenever possible we used to go on weekends for sightseeing to explore new areas or for a day out or for picnics. Amongst some of our favourite places to visit were going to Hyde Park for boating in Serpentine Lake or to Cambridge for punting in the river or for a trip to the scenic town of Stratford upon Avon, Shakespeare's birthplace. We would also go to some of these places with our friends and families who came from overseas. On long weekends, we would extend the visits to Lake District and stop over at Oxford University on our way back, visit the historic town of Bath, etc. On our longer family holidays, we covered Cornwall, Cheddar Gorge and many other destinations.

On our first visit Veena, I and Maneesh went to the Lake District, and made our base at Lake Windermere. Lake District holds the status of the World Heritage Site and we wanted to explore all its beautiful scenery, its lakes and Scafell Pike, the highest (point) mountain in England. We set out on our journey after breakfast. We started with a boat ride in Lake Windermere and had an opportunity to do a photo shoot on our way to Lake Coniston Water. Our next visit was to Lake Wast Water. We realised it was beginning to get dark and we needed to find a place to stay. So, we started looking for a hotel. We came across a number of small hotels and bed and breakfast places but they were all fully occupied.

While searching, we saw a gentleman pottering about in his front lawn and asked him if there were any good hotels nearby. He directed us to one just a bit further up but with a warning that at this time of the year it may be full too. To our disappointment, that is how it turned out to be. On our way back as we were driving past the same gentleman, he waved at me to stop and asked me to pull over in his front drive. Asking us to follow him inside the house, he showed us a bedroom. He said that he lived all alone in the house and had this spare bedroom, which he would be happy to give to us. In fact, he insisted we stay in it saying that he could not let us wander around at that time of the night in the hope of finding a place. We were delighted with the genuine offer and decided to stay there. It was a lovely cottage that backed on to the coastline. He served a simple meal after which we sat down and chatted late into the night – mostly about India. As we found out later, he retired as a headmaster and had come across a number of Indian students who had developed his fascination for India. He served us a healthy breakfast next morning and as we were leaving, I asked him what I should pay him. He absolutely declined my offer to pay. However, on my insistence he agreed to take a couple of quid for the laundry. We moved on from there to Scafell Pike and some other lakes and back to our hotel. We stayed in touch with this gentleman for quite a few years exchanging Xmas cards.

We were also booked on a holiday to Cotswolds by our children, where we stayed at a quirky little hotel which had each room done in a different décor representing different eras of British kingdom. This was another enjoyable experience.

We always wanted to explore Scotland, Wales and Ireland, the three countries that in addition to England constituted the United Kingdom. Our first visit was to Inverness, the largest city and the cultural capital of the Scottish Highlands. Its old town features 19th century Inverness Cathedral and there is Inverness Museum and the Art Gallery, which trace the history of the Highland. Apart from these, there is not really much to see in Inverness. We enjoyed going round on long drives to enjoy the beautiful highland scenery. We also went on a day's picnic to the Loch Ness but unfortunately did not see Nessie, the mythical monster.

While visiting Wales, we decided to make Neath located on the river by the same name in South Wales, as our base. From here, we could explore the many picturesque valleys and small old mining communities. Another key attraction was the Brecon Beacons national park. Being close to the coastline, there were also a number of beaches that we had access to. One pleasant incident from our visit to Tenby beach sticks in my memory. We were relaxing on the beach when I noticed some people doing parascending. It immediately caught my fancy but I thought Veena and Sasha would not be too keen on trying it. So, I decided to go for it telling them that I needed to go to the restroom. I found the operator of parascending as he was just about to close for lunch. However, I managed to persuade him to take me for a ride before he closed. I did my parascending and thoroughly enjoyed it. When I returned to the beach, Sasha pointed to the people parascending. This is when I told them that I had just done it and asked Sasha if she had seen me too.

Following my experience, Sasha and Maneesh also showed keenness on doing parascending. So, we decided to take a weekend trip to Bournemouth where they had the facility for doing it. In UK, when you are parascending, they don you with a life jacket and strap you in a seat that is at the end of a rope that is attached to a winch on a boat. As the boat moves and starts to gain speed, the parachute attached to your seat lifts up and they start releasing the rope, which lifts you up in the air. One thing they tell you is that if there is an accident, the boat will stop and you will start coming down. You have to release yourself from the parachute when you are close to water and a boat will come and pick you up. All of us boarded the boat and I was the first one to go for parascending and thoroughly enjoyed it. Maneesh followed me and also had a wonderful experience. Now it was Sasha's turn and they decided to play a little prank on her. When she was quite high, they slowed down the boat and started calling out to her saying that the engine had failed. This started to bring Sasha down and her feet began to skim the water. But before she could undo her parachute, they sped the boat again lifting her up in the air. Although initially scared, Sasha thoroughly enjoyed the prank and the whole experience. Finally, it was Veena's turn next and after a bit of resistance she was persuaded to go for it and came out exhilarated like all of us.

Our next trip was to Northern Ireland where I had to go on a two-day official visit for implementation of the largest Sainsbury's supermarket in Ballymena. I decided to extend the visit over the weekend and took Veena with me. Northern Ireland is well known for its unhurried pace of life and of course its pubs. We enjoyed the ride through the Glens exuding its own scenic charm. A visit to Giants Causeway, a UNESCO world heritage site, where the polygonal-shaped natural stone features (some 40000 of them) were created by a volcanic eruption some 60 million years ago, was an amazing treat for the eyes.

With my love for driving, we never got to travel to many places by train. One exception to this was our trip on Eurostar to Paris to attend the wedding of one of our friend's son. The wedding took place in a chateau in France while the Indian wedding ceremony was held in the open under a tree, which created a marvellous scene on this beautiful sunny day. Madhuri Dixit was one of the invitees to the wedding but was unable to make it due to her prior commitments. However, we managed to meet her father-in-law and mother-in-law at the wedding.

Besides travelling, we also liked to go out to eat in London. Two of our favourite places that served the best dosas in those days were Diwana near Euston Station, and Woodlands. We also liked Bombay Palace and Agra restaurant at Gaylord for its quality and selection of vegetarian dishes. In fact, I took my ICL colleagues to Gaylord around one Christmas and they thoroughly enjoyed the food. I also took a group of senior managers from Sainsbury's and from ICL Sales and Customer Services team to Bombay Palace who enlisted me with their corporate club membership. On special occasions, we would also visit the high-end restaurants. For instance, when Maneesh made announcement of his proposal of marriage and later fatherhood, we went to Banaras, which is the only Michelin star Indian restaurant in London. We also visited Veeraswamy for one of the birthday celebrations and The Ritz for high tea for one of our wedding anniversaries.

Maneesh's Education:

As Maneesh was reaching the age of moving to senior school, we had a decision to make. If he would clear the eleven plus examination, we would send him to the Grammar School. If not, we would have to send him to a private school. He appeared for the entrance exams for two private schools near us and also for the eleven plus exam for selection to the Grammar School. He was offered a place with scholarship at one of the private schools (Forest School) and also got through the eleven plus exam to make him eligible for the Grammar School. When we visited the Forest School, they talked to us about our background and other details. Then they suggested if we would accept if they gave Maneesh half the scholarship and offer the other half to another student. Maneesh however expressed his preference to go to the Grammar School and we decided to go for it.

Ilford County High was in an area called Clayhall, some 4-5 miles away from our house. As we had also been thinking about changing the house, this presented us an ideal opportunity to move to Clayhall and we bought our next house there.

The next big milestone in Maneesh's life came in 1986 when he had to make a choice of the subject and the university he wanted to go to. Between Oxford and Cambridge, you were only allowed to select one. Maneesh chose Cambridge and also some other universities that formed a part of university selection procedure. He had decided that he definitely did not want to go for medicine and chose Economics instead. To utmost delight of all of us, he got the offer of a place from Churchill College at Cambridge to study economics. Churchill College was well renowned for its Economics department and Maneesh accepted the offer happily.

Sasha's Milestones:

A few years later it was Sasha's turn to move to secondary school and we went through the same process again. She sailed through the eleven plus exam for a place at Woodford County High School.

Like Maneesh, Sasha also planned to go to Cambridge for her university and got an offer from St John's College. However, she was very disappointed when the Economics paper for the A Level exams was so much adrift from the curriculum that they had covered. This resulted in her missing her place at Cambridge and she decided to go to Manchester University instead.

For her 21st birthday celebration, Sasha was very keen to have a big party and we decided to hire the Laguna Banqueting Hall for the same. We had a large gathering of friends and family and everyone thoroughly enjoyed the day with good food and lots of music to dance to.

Social Life

We had developed a large circle of friends that made for a very active, interesting and pleasant social life. Our friendship with Vijay and Rajshree expanded to a large group with friends and 'friends of friends' joining the group over time. Our active involvement in Jain Association made us a part of this large group of members who met fairly frequently. We had also carried forward our contacts with my IIT batch mates who had come to settle in the UK. Many of the connections from all of above became family friends sharing in the celebrations of family occasions like weddings, birthdays etc.

My involvement in Samarpan music group presented opportunities for going out for meals, to attend concerts by renowned artists and even giving our musical performance at a number of events. My membership of couple of bridge clubs and the fact that I arranged 'bridge weekends' in Worthing also added to good social outings. Even my yoga teachers training group was a good source of social activity.

During early years I had abstained from playing *teen-patti* apart from an odd social occasion. However, in the later part of our life we got involved in a couple of kitty parties where the focus was on teen-patti and these had become quite a regular affair. We would get together, have a drink and snacks and then spend a good few hours playing cards and then finish with a meal and a chat. We played with stakes such that it encouraged everyone to take the game seriously but kept them low for us not to feel bad about the loss at the end of the game.

A Memorable Incident of My Life

Mr Modi made his first official visit to UK in November 2015. He was warmly received by the British Government as well as the Indian diaspora. A huge celebration was held in his honour at the Wembley Stadium, which was filled to capacity. He was even accompanied to the event by Prime Minister David Cameron. Following the celebration, there was a dinner reception hosted by the High Commission of India (HCI) in Sir Bobby Moore Hall. I had the honour of being invited to the dinner and had an opportunity of getting a group photo taken with Mr Modi. However, this was the day when the terrorist attack took place in Paris and on receiving this news, Mr Modi decided to leave immediately from there.

One key and perhaps the most important part of my family life is the holidays that we have enjoyed with family and friends. Apart from a few that I have mentioned earlier, I have covered these later in the book under 'A Lifetime of Holidays'.

A big thank you:

We are really thankful to all our family and friends who joined on this journey of life with us and help make it a wonderful experience.

4. Professional life

INTERNATIONAL COMPUTERS LIMITED (ICL)

I had a very successful, satisfying and enjoyable career with ICL that lasted 30 years. The few twists and turns in between make it all the more interesting.

I was to begin work on 22 June 1970. My employment letter directed me to report to the Regional Manager of the Customer Services Unit in number 29-31 on Farringdon Street which was not far from my home.

I dressed up in my best suit for the first day at work, reached Farringdon Street and started looking for number 29-31. Initially, I went past the address and returned to find a small entrance leading to a narrow passage and stairs leading up to an open plan office. I was a bit disappointed seeing it as the main ICL building in Putney where my interview was held and even the ICT building in Delhi were much grander. As I entered the office, Alan Roberts, one of the Service Managers, approached me and I presented my joining letter to him. He informed me that the Regional Manager was not in office that morning and directed me to join a team of engineers who were carrying out maintenance at Barclays computer centre in Euston. I reached the location and was asked by the engineer in charge to join another engineer in the maintenance of a card punch. If someone has seen a card punch on a PDP system, he would know it is not the most exciting thing one would want to do dressed in the best suit. During break, we had a chat about the system we were working on. I also mentioned that I wanted to work as a systems engineer on ICL's 1900 systems. The engineer-in-charge informed me that it may be possible only after 5-6 years and that too only if I was able to prove myself to be one of the top engineers. My immediate reaction was "did I come all the way to London to work on these machines". I decided to go back and informed the team leader that I may return to the office after finishing the maintenance.

When I reached the office later that day, the Regional Manager was in and I requested to see him. After talking to me and going through my appointment letter, he asked me to wait. A while later, he came in with Gary Thomas and introduced us to each other. He also told me that I would be working under Gary who looked after 1900 systems in London. Gary was a Welsh gentleman, well spoken and nicely dressed. He spent some time with me, made a few phone calls and told me that I was to go to the Costain's site in Lambeth North next morning. I met Don, the site engineer at Costain's next morning who was a very experienced engineer. It did not take me very long to realize why I was placed there considering it was not a particularly large site. Don was a very keen betting man. His daily routine included a visit to the betting shop soon after tea break in the morning and then go to review the results and collect his winning in the afternoon. On a good win, he would also pop in for a quick pint on the way back. Good thing was that he did not mind me taking greater charge of the site. This gave me an opportunity to start arranging the spares and technical manuals and improve general upkeep of the site. Costain Group was a very large builder in London and had another office near our building which also housed a canteen. We normally went there for lunch and this is where I departed from my vegetarian diet. At the canteen, the choice for me was a cheese sandwich on Monday, and the same on the next day and again the same the day after. Soon I began trying egg preparations to offer me some choice. I started enjoying the omelettes that added some variety to my meals and gradually I started taking other items as well.

There are some incidents of my past that I still remember and would like to mention here. The first one was with a good friend of mine who joined at the same time as me. He was always smartly dressed in a suit and a tie and had a typical stiff upper-lip attitude. One very hot sunny day, on our way to the canteen I asked him if he did not feel uncomfortable in the suit. He replied very firmly, "It is not proper to take your jacket off in public". His reply amused me but I kept quiet.

Another incident worth quoting was with an engineer-in-charge at one of the sites. I was the only Indian in our team of engineers. Although I would not say that I experienced any discrimination at ICL but there can be odd incident of bias by individuals. We had an equipment maintenance schedule for all the sites in our patch and a group of us would visit the sites to carry out the routine maintenance work. The most notorious equipment in the list was line printers that made our hands very messy. This task was usually delegated to the junior engineers and as a novice I had already done my fair share of work on these. However, one day we had a schedule of two sites for maintenance, one in the morning and one in the afternoon. I did my share of maintenance on a line printer in the morning and went to the second site. There I was handed over the maintenance schedule for two printers by the engineer-in-charge, which I refused to accept. I told him that I already had my fair share of these and someone else should take charge of one of them.

Image that will conjure up in reader's mind of a printer is that of a small box that sits on the desk and what could be so distasteful about cleaning one? What I am talking about were the floor-standing ones, much like a printing machine. Used with corporate systems, these would print continuous stationery at the speed of 1600 lines per minute with the line width of up to 160 characters. These were a little marvel of engineering.

Back to the story, the engineer-in-charge was not very happy with my attitude and I could sense the feeling of 'British ruled India' in his eyes. He retorted by saying, "Who will do these then"? I did not say anything to him but the team leader who was also there grasped the situation and took one of the sheets from me saying he would take care of it.

Shift working:

After some experience on the systems, I joined shift working that involved working in the evening and night shifts in rotation with the usual day shift. It was a welcome opportunity as it added a decent premium to the salary. In the evening shifts, we were mainly involved in support calls, which gave me an opportunity to build my skills on a wide range of equipment. It was a bit daunting initially as we were working totally on our own. There was one engineer in the evening shifts that had a reputation of being very fast at fixing a fault. However, very often there were repeat calls for the same fault. We were all aware of this and the service desk would normally tell us that the fault being passed on to us had already been attended to by this engineer.

The night shifts were primarily planned to carry out routine maintenance on the systems where the customer was not willing to release the system during daytime. Our schedule of maintenance for one of these nights included Bank of England followed by Hospital Computer Centre (HCC). One night I left Bank of England for HCC with two other engineers sharing the car with me. Both these engineers happened to be quite tall and big build and we were also carrying our tool kits in the boot of the car. As we came to pass Hyde Park Corner, we were followed by a police car and signalled to stop. One officer came to my side and asked me to lower the window and "what was the purpose of our journey". I told him that we were coming from Bank of England and going to Hospital Computer Centre. A quizzical appearance came upon his face that 'either I was being facetious or what could we be doing at Bank of England at 1am in the night' and he signalled his colleague to come over. While he was talking to me, the other officer asked my friend on the passenger side to come out and open the boot of the car. The officer saw the tool kits in the boot and asked my friend to show his ID to reconfirm our story. They were obviously satisfied with our story and let us go.

Another site on our list was the computer centre for the Islington Town Hall. It was quite a large installation and the customer had provided a big room to the site engineer who had put up a dartboard in the room. One evening I arrived rather early and there was no one at the site. Although I had played darts a few times during our visits to the pub but I wasn't much good at it. However, I decided to have a go and concentrating hard at the bull's eye I said to myself, "What if I hit the bull's eye!" and threw the dart. It surprised me when I hit it. And once again I said, "What if I hit it again!" and I did hit it. This time I was totally aghast and said, "Could I really hit it the third time?" and as if by magic, I hit it the third time. I am sure I must have jumped a few times with excitement and left the darts in the board. As soon as the first engineer arrived, I showed him the dartboard and told him that I had actually hit those. He laughed, took the darts out, moved to the throwing line and slowly moved forward towards the board planting the three darts in the bull's eye saying this is how it is done.

Team Leader:

A few years later I was promoted to be a team leader and was allocated a team of engineers and 7 customers in London. It was a mix of customers varying from HCC, Electricity Board, and Metropolitan Police to three of London Boroughs computer installations. This provided me an excellent opportunity to develop my man management as well as customer liaison skills and I thoroughly enjoyed the experience. Metropolitan Police had one major computer centre in Putney, which did most of their office cum administrative work, and another one in Portman Square in Central London, which managed the traffic tickets. Those were the days of computer cards where the traffic tickets were transferred to punched cards and once read into the system, the whole process of sending notices, monitoring payments and issuing warrants on no-payment were carried out by the system. As a part of my regular visits, I happened to visit the site one day after I had just been issued a traffic ticket (now referred to as PCN) a few days ago. In general conversation, I mentioned this to the Operations Team Leader and he asked me to give the ticket to him and not to worry about it. A couple of days later we had a call from the site to our service desk reporting a wreck on their card reader. An engineer was sent to the site to fix the problem. Anyway, I never heard anything more about my ticket. Perhaps a few other recipients of PCNs also got their tickets written off.

My Customer Services Manager had a quirky hobby of keeping all his customer files at close hand so that he could access them without moving from his desk. Those days all files were in paper form. He achieved his objective by stacking all the files into a number of piles on his desk. As a result, one could hardly see his desk. One day I needed to get a letter from him that was received from Metropolitan Police. He immediately went to one of the piles and rummaging through it he took out the relevant file and gave me the letter. He then kept the file back onto the pile after marking the place from where the letter had come. It amazed me how he kept track of which file was in which pile.

It was in late seventies that ICL launched its new range of mainframe systems under the banner of 2900 series. These systems also came with a new operating system known as Virtual Machine Environment (VME). As the name implied, it helped to make all the resources of the whole system available to any application that was running concurrently on the system. The result was that a larger number of applications could be run simultaneously without being limited by the total size of the system and without loss of performance. This was truly a remarkable jump in the processing power and I still feel sometimes that ICL did not advertise enough to exploit these system's full potential. Having worked as an engineer for quite some time and looking at the design of the hardware architecture and the quality of the component parts made me realise how technologically advanced UK was at that time.

First Visit to US:

Our first visit to USA was in 1978 and we stayed with my brother-in-law Dharam in New York. We did most of the sightseeing around New York and New Jersey. During the visit Dharam suggested to us to move to US and I decided to look for an opportunity. I found an advertisement for systems engineers and decided to go for an interview at Burroughs Corporation. I was made an offer of a job on the spot. However, as I had no green card, they assured me that if I wished to accept the offer they would get it sorted. I came back to UK after our holidays leaving them to work on it.

Kuwait Assignment and Experience:

After about a year of returning from US, I came across an opportunity in ICL to work on an assignment as a support engineer in Kuwait. We were to commission one of our new range 2960 systems for the Kuwait Oil Company (KOC). I had mixed feelings about accepting the position as going to Kuwait meant having much greater responsibility to fix all problems without any immediate support that is normally available in UK. At the same time that I was considering this offer, totally out of the blue, I received a call from Burroughs (reference our visit to USA in 1978) to inform me that they had all the paperwork ready for me to join them. However, between the family we decided to go to Kuwait.

This turned out to be a really good chapter in our life. The package offered included a significant supplement for working overseas as well as free accommodation and living expenses in Kuwait. We found that we could live very comfortably within the allowances in Kuwait and save all our UK salary.

I had gone as a part of ICL's project team to commission and support their corporate system and also train the engineers on site for ongoing support. We were provided accommodation in a lavish 2-bedroom apartment in Fahaheel, a town just a short distance from Ahmadi, the base of KOC. All project team members from ICL were treated as senior managers and had access to all the facilities of KOC including their social and sports facilities at Hubara Centre. The project team bonded very well forgetting their usual British reserve, and would drop on each other for a drink or a meal without invitation. We would also go for frequent outings to the clubs, beaches and other places. Talking of the drink, when my wife came to join me a few days later I asked her to bring a bottle of Scotch with her. At the airport when they asked her if she had anything to declare, she told them about the whiskey. They just inquired about me and my work in Kuwait and when she told them that I was a part of the British team working for KOC, they let her go with the bottle.

The system was delivered soon after our arrival to Kuwait and we set out to commission it. One incident at an early stage during the installation process brought my fears to life. I tested the processor and the storage unit (memory) thoroughly before moving them to their designated positions. Soon after, we found that intermittent failures were being picked in the memory. However, we persevered and discovered that it was due to a missing cable, which is used to ground the storage unit. It had been missed by the factory and the fault was obscured as the two units were in physical contact with each other during earlier testing. After this, the whole installation was completed without any further incidents and the system was handed over to the customer on schedule.

A few months later some more Exchangeable Disc Systems (EDS) were delivered which were to be added to the configuration. After some time, one of the EDS started exhibiting an intermittent fault. The project manager was aware that this unit had an accident while being unloaded from the ship and had made an insurance claim for it. These were expensive machines worth around £30,000 and I discussed with the project manager if we could try to fix the fault locally. One weekend, accompanied by another support engineer, I went to investigate the fault. The project team was due to meet the same evening for a meal at the nightclub at Hilton Hotel. We managed to find the fault that was a break in the voice-coil. This was a highly sophisticated mechanism and could only be replaced in the factory. This is what would have happened if it were in the UK. But the two of us decided to use our ingenuity and fix the break in the coil ourselves. Fortunately, it worked and we tested the disc drive thoroughly with rigorous engineering tests and it passed. When we joined the rest of the project team in the evening, the project manager was more than delighted to have made this saving. It was surprising for me to realize how much you can achieve when you do not draw boundaries around you.

After successful completion of the project, the project manager wanted to throw a party to celebrate and hand over the system to KOC. As it would involve drinks, he discussed it with his counterpart in KOC and they agreed to hold the party in a marquee in Ahmadi. Since there were senior KOC managers with us at the party, there were no restrictions on drinks and we had a wonderful time.

We had access to a number of pool cars provided by ICL for our personal use. But I had decided beforehand to have my own car and bought a Buick Regal. It was in connection with this car that I was visiting the dealership where I happened to meet an Indian employee of KOC. He was also from UK and was working as a manager in Kuwait. He invited me to meet his family and his circle of friends who were all from India and working as senior managers. They were a nice bunch of people and this meeting opened up a huge opportunity for us to socialise and enjoy life in Kuwait.

Our social life was very exciting and enjoyable with the two groups that we were part of – ICL project team and our Indian social circle. We would go frequently for outings or visit Hubara centre where we had access to a high-quality restaurant, swimming, tennis and a lot of other sports. We also had squash courts in our apartment block and a rooftop swimming pool, which was more or less like our private family pool. Veena also took to squash and quite enjoyed it. Maneesh joined the International School and was very good at studies coming first in his class. We also enjoyed shopping in Kuwait as we would feel comfortable buying what we liked rather than being restricted by its price.

On an overseas assignment we were allowed a paid trip to our hometown in UK. Instead of travelling to UK, we decided to make a trip to India and visit my sister in Mumbai (then Bombay). Our children being of similar age group enjoyed each other's company and had a good time together. We travelled around Mumbai and also visited the historic world heritage site of Ellora and Ajanta. The caves there depict Hindu, Buddhist and Jain religious work in the form of architecture and paintings. Some of them looked so fresh as if they had only been painted recently. The architecture of rock-cut-temple of Kailashnath was totally mesmerising. Even to date the archaeologists are puzzled by how this magnitude of work could have been done in those days without technology and the time it would have taken to carve out the temple structure out of a mountain.

Prohibition of liquor in Kuwait was a rather loosely enforced regulation but we were always cautious of not flaunting the same openly. I remember one incident of our visit to a nightclub in one of the top hotels. Using our normal caution of ladies carrying gin in their water bottles and gents hiding and carrying bottles of whisky in a bag, we sat down at our table. As we got ready for dinner, the project manager started pouring drinks in glasses under the table and passed them around. Suddenly we noticed a group of Germans walking in and plonking their bottles of drinks on their table and drinking freely. Perhaps it was our British reserve that we still maintained the 'hide the bottles under the table' policy.

Another interesting incident took place when I went to the golf club in Ahmadi with a couple of friends. As we sat down in the clubhouse, my friend went to the counter and shouted from there to know what we wanted for drinks. One of us jokingly said, "A pint of lager please!" and the other one shouted back, "A gin and tonic please". We were all puzzled to hear him repeat the order at the counter and coming back with our drinks. We found out later that it was one place in Kuwait where you could order and get any drink you wanted.

It seems strange when I think that we were in Kuwait only for about 15-16 months. We had such a wonderful time there that we wanted to extend our stay there. An opportunity did appear for me to replace the engineer-in-charge who was due to come back to UK. However, my regional manager did not agree to extend my stay as he wanted me back for a particular role in London.

Engineer-in-charge at J Sainsbury's:

The role that regional manager wanted me to take over was of the engineer-in-charge at Sainsbury's. It was ICL's largest retail customer and a prestigious client. I had no hesitation in accepting the offer. There was a very experienced engineer based at the site but his attitude left a lot to be desired. A number of service managers had tried to correct his ways to no avail. He had a problem with drinking and would only be found in the pub after midday until closing time (which was around 3:30 pm those days). He happened to be very close to the customer's site manager hence no one wanted to upset the relationship. Once the current systems manager called him to say that he wanted to see him to discuss a problem and was told, "Why don't we meet at 'Rose and Crown' (the local public house) in the afternoon". This made the regional manager take a decision of bringing me in.

I visited the site and was amazed to see the size of the computer room, which was like a quarter of a football field. Sainsbury's had one of ICLs flagship dual processor 2980 system and a wide range of peripherals. Fortunately for me, the customer's site manager left soon after and was replaced by a new manager with whom I developed a very good rapport. Soon we were also able to retire our offending site engineer (who left voluntarily) and we started to build a healthy relationship with the customer.

Due to the importance and potential of growth of JS's business, the company had appointed a Customer Service (CS) account manager who was also based on the site. Together we built a very good relationship with the customer, steadily improving our performance and the level of customer satisfaction.

As the leading information technology company, ICL kept abreast with the technological developments around the world that we could explore and exploit for the development of our customer's business. One such technology was the laser scanning equipment that would significantly improve the efficiency of the process of checkout. The challenge here was to produce a very light and thin mirrored concave glass disc that could be spun at a very fast speed without shattering. All major players like IBM, HP and Fujitsu were working on a solution but Fujitsu was the first one to come up with a working solution. I was invited to attend a presentation being given to a group of managers from ICL. A group consisting of a designer, a software developer and some other people from Fujitsu in Japan were to make this presentation. They demonstrated the scanner and gave a brief overview of the algorithm that converted the scanned data to the bar code of the product. The challenge here was that the checkout operator could present the product to the scanner at any angle and facing in any direction and the algorithm had to take care of all that. The software developer showed us the copy of the algorithm, which was like two large copies of encyclopaedia. The scanners were eventually bought by Sainsbury's and installed in all their existing and future stores.

Just to give you another example, there was another technological solution developed for the prevention of pilferage from the stores, which was a huge problem for the business. The solution consisted of a very small diode that would be attached alongside the barcode on all the high-value products. There was a high intensity scanner built inside the main barcode scanner that would burst this diode when the item was scanned at the checkout. As the customer walked out of the store, he would pass between scanning equipment that would be looking for the presence of any undisturbed diode and an alarm signal would go if there was one detected. The security guard at the store would then intercept the customer and take appropriate action on confirmation of the intact diode. This was implemented for trial in some of the stores but was discarded, as it was not a very cost effective and viable solution.

Systems Service Manager:

After spending a few years at Sainsbury's, I applied for the vacancy of Systems Service Manager (SSM) in the Retail Service division and was selected for the post. I was allocated the Central London patch with a team of 51 engineers and three Distributed Engineering Managers (DEM). I found this to be a very good team with a mix of some younger engineers, mainly working as Customer Service Representatives (CSR) and other engineers including some specialists and support engineers. I also had the responsibility of the Customer Service Desk, which provided centralised support to all retail teams in the country. CSRs were equipped with a company van and would carry high use spares in it. These engineers would cover a large number of routine calls in a day with a very high hit rate. They would replenish their vans or parts not available in the van from our central spares depot in London.

My customer base could not have been more diverse with customers from most of the Government departments like Health and Social Security (DHSS), Her Majesty's Income Tax (HMIT), Department of Education (DOE), Home Office, Cabinet Office a number of financial institutions like Barclays, Warburg Securities, a number of London Boroughs (L B Wandsworth, L B Lambeth), Metropolitan Police and Ministry of Defence and major stores like Marks and Spencer's, Sainsbury's and Waitrose.

I always tried to develop a clear and honest understanding with my team of engineers and team leaders. We made a number of service improvements and were high up in the delivery of measures across the retail teams in the country. One such improvement was that each DEM would spend the last hour of his time in going through the calls on the service desk for his own patch and plan the necessary actions for the following day. I also found that the improvement actions usually came from the people on the lower rung of the ladder. They were the ones who were handling things hands on. One such suggestion came from a young service desk representative. She explained that a number of hours of the CSR's were wasted in the morning when they went to pick up their orders from the stores. She suggested that we place next morning's orders on the system on previous evening and the stores could pick these and keep them ready for the CSRs. This made tremendous sense and I set up a meeting with the stores manager to agree with the process and arrange to have an allocated area for CSR to pick their orders without delay. As we had a large team of CSRs in the team, this saving of time made a huge improvement in our performance figures.

One major event that had a significant impact on retail system teams across the country was the acquisition of the service contract for HMIT (Inland Revenue). It was a very large contract and came with very strict performance targets with penalties for non-conformance. The CS director was absolutely delighted about winning this contract and also made it his personal mission to ensure delivery of the service to meet the targets. He instructed all managers about this and set up a procedure wherein every incident of non-conformance was to be reported to him on a daily basis. And on a repeat incident of a non-conformance in the same team within a month, the line manager was to report to him personally.

This was conveyed very clearly to all my teams with a further instruction to the service desk to inform of any incident from HMIT to the relevant DEM who must ensure its proper management. If an incident came within half an hour of the target time, I was to be informed about it. The process worked very well and we avoided any failures. However, there was one incident when the engineers working on the fault fixed it in time but reported the closure after feeding the meter of their parked car to avoid paying a parking ticket. According to the service desk system, this was classified as a non-conformance. I discussed the situation with the customer's manager who accepted that the system had been handed back to them within the prescribed time. He also agreed to make this correction on our system. However, I was not at all happy with the situation and asked the engineers to come to the office.

After the engineers explained everything, I just told them that if they were ever in such a situation in future, they must ensure that they clear the call on time and if there was a parking ticket to be paid, I will cover it. I think the message got around well among the teams and we never had a single non-conformance on any of our sites again. All the engineers became very alert to these calls and offered any help they could to an engineer working on these incidents to make sure of compliance.

Our CS director had just one chart in his office that showed the performance of all teams across the country on calls from HMIT. My team was the only one that had no entries against it. My Customer Services Manager (CSM) once told me that in a meeting with the director a CSM from another region raised the issue of larger distances to travel in their area to which the director retorted by saying, "Have you ever driven in Central London and looked for a place to park there". The CSM did not know what to say after that.

There is a funny incident that I would like to include here. ICL implemented a Quality program across the company where all staff from ground up to senior managers were mandated to undergo this training. It so happened that I attended the very last session of this training program. As such, the editor of the ICL quarterly magazine had come to the event, accompanied with a photographer, to publish the successful completion of the program in the magazine. At the end of the session the editor asked the instructor to provide the names of all the students and he gave my name as JD. The editor said "I can't publish JD, do you know his first name". He was told that 'no, we all know him only as JD'.

Now, I need to provide a bit of background here. British like to anglicise the first names of all foreigners pretending that they find it difficult to pronounce our names. When I joined ICL and introduced myself, I was told "can we call you John". I said no, but if you find it difficult to pronounce my name, you can call me by my initials JD. Since then I came to be known as JD wherever I travelled to ICL's offices around the country.

When the magazine came out, my name under the photo appeared as 'Jaydee' courtesy an ingenious translation by the editor. A few months later, I happened to give a presentation to a room full of managers in the presence of our Customer Services Director. For the presentation, I had prepared my introduction page with a flap with my name JD Jain on it and Jaydee written under the flap. I started the presentation light heartedly by saying, "I am J D Jain and not Jaydee (lifting the flap at the same time) as some people would like you to believe." The director fell about laughing knowing fully well what I was referring to. The editor happened to be in the room as well and did not know which way to turn.

Project Manager at Chase Bank:

One morning I got a call from the Regional Head's secretary saying that he wanted to see me. He explained that he wanted to see me directly before talking to my CS Manager.

He also said that he would talk to the manager only if I was happy with the proposal he was making to me. He continued by saying that he had heard a lot about my problem-solving skills and there was something for which he needed my help. There was an ongoing intermittent fault at Chase Bank where our system was being used for 'online trading'. It was the system sold by him in his earlier role as Sales Manager. The customer had become aware of the ongoing problem and was rather concerned. He wanted me to take over as the Project Manager for the site to get an urgent solution to the problem. He promised to provide me full support in whatever way I needed. He further explained that this was the only ICL system that had been sold for online trading and if there were a major incident, it would seriously jeopardise our sales in that market segment. On my agreeing, he introduced me to the customer Operations Manager and arranged for my CSM to relieve me of my current responsibilities. I visited the site and met with the customer's Operations Manager. I also had a meeting with our site-based engineers and the senior support engineer. I wanted the engineers to give me full update on the type of system, nature of fault, result of diagnostics information so far and the potential area of fault. The support engineer explained that it was a dual processor system where the two processors worked in sync with each other in a master and slave arrangement. If there was a fault in the master, processing would automatically transfer to the slave without any interruption to the service and any knowledge to the customer. The system would automatically produce a software dump of the incident, which would be analysed by the support engineers to help identify the fault and take corrective action at a suitable time. The dual system would be restored during reload at night. A small risk in the whole process was that if the slave developed a fault while the master was out of action due to an earlier incident, it would lead to a crash and complete shutdown.

Unfortunately, the customer's Operations Manager was an ex-ICL salesman and was fully aware of this danger. The support engineer informed me that from the diagnosis of the dumps, the fault seemed to be in one of the memory boards. As rigorous testing of the memory had not identified the fault, a possible course of action was to replace a number of boards at a time and eliminate the fault. However, there were 16 such boards in each system and even if we acquired all the boards in the spares loop it would take us at least 4 attempts. There was also a high risk with this approach. The boards in the spares loop could not be entirely relied upon. When I asked the support engineer what was the guaranteed way to fix the problem as quickly as possible, he said half-jokingly, "If I could get them 16 new boards, it would fix the problem immediately".

I decided to call our factory in Ashton under Lyne and spoke to Jim Brohy, the test and quality assurance manager. I explained the situation to him and asked if there was any possibility of getting 16 new boards. During the conversation I came to know that there was a system undergoing soak test and was due to go to a customer in five days. But there was no way he would agree to release these boards. I asked him, "Jim tell me who is one person in the company who can authorise you to take these boards out of the machine?" He went quiet for a while and then said, "JD, I can let you have these boards but you must promise me to collect the boards tomorrow and return the other boards to me definitely by Sunday". I could not wait to say yes to him and arranged with the engineering team to carry out the work on Saturday morning. The task was completed in the morning and a thorough testing of the machine was carried out the whole day without any incidents.

I went to return the boards on Sunday and asked Jim what had made him change his mind to release the boards. He said, "JD this has never happened before in the history of ICL. But when I heard the passion in your voice, I just could not say no. We both work for the same company after all!"

We had no further incidents and I went to see the regional manager and told him the whole story. He asked me, "If Jim had asked you to call Peter Bonfield (our Chairman at that time), would you have called him?" I gently reminded him that he had told me I had his full support and we left it at that.

CHOTS Project:

ICL was making a bid for the Ministry of Defence's (MoD) project for Computerisation of Head Offices Technology Systems (CHOTS). Our main competition was IBM who had already developed and delivered such a system to the American defence establishment. The question was whether the ministry would opt for an already tried and tested solution or would it be willing to give its own IT industry a chance to develop a system to meet its requirements and also be able to offer it at a competitive price. A central project team headed by a Project Director was set up and Customer Services were asked to nominate people to the team to work on our part of the bid. A Customer Service Manager from South East Region was elected and I was to work with him to help in this role. The CSM attended a few meetings in the beginning but then decided that I was quite capable of handling this on my own and he withdrew from the team.

The project was a five-year phased implementation programme of the MoD's offices across the country. Regular meetings were held with the team from MoD to discuss the requirements, the schedule of rollout, the performance criteria and the targets for service level. The requirements also included specific security measures for which we had to develop new technology in some of our equipment. After months of hard work and diligence, we finally won the contract, which was worth around £750 million. This was the largest and the most prestigious contract that ICL had ever won.

The team started working on producing the procedures and other documentation in line with the requirements of MoD. I visited all the CS regional headquarters and gave presentations detailing the phased roll out programme, the security requirements, our service strategy and the targets for service delivery and procedures. The line managers were asked to prepare their teams for the project and provide the list for me to get their security clearances. I also presented the Customer Service's cost-model to the senior executives for their approval and received the same.

We were having regular meetings with very senior people in MoD. Due to the level of MoD people I was having meetings with (at Principal level) and also considering my area of responsibility, it was decided that I should be promoted to Senior Management. I was put through the assessment centre and came out successful, resulting in my promotion.

We were handling classified information on the project and hence had been security vetted and provided with relevant IDs. There were strict guidelines to follow including giving advance information to the project team about our destination and about the duration if we were going out of the country; not to leave any such documentation in the car and keep it under lock and key in the house if we were carrying any such information with us.

While it was all going smooth at work, I had a little unpleasant incident as I returned home one day. I parked the car outside the house and as I put the key in the door of the house to open it, I could hear Veena and Sasha running up to the door and opening it from inside. At the same time, I heard a voice from behind and saw a young man standing behind me asking for instructions to get to Ilford. I moved out to the kerb and started giving him directions but noticed that he kept looking at my face and seemed not to be following my instructions. Next thing I knew was that he was holding me from behind with his hand around my throat asking me for the keys of the car. He told me not to do anything clever as he had a knife to my stomach. I quickly shouted out to my wife and daughter in Hindi to lock the door from inside and not to come out. I handed the keys to the chap. He took them and threw them to another chap who had appeared by the side of the car in the meantime. The first chap just pushed me the floor and asked me to hand over the wallet as well, which I did. Within no time, they just drove off with my car.

I came inside the house and reported the incident to the police who inquired about any injuries or anything serious. When I said there were no serious injuries apart from falling on the ground, they just informed me that they will file a report and that seemed to be the end of the matter. My family was badly shaken by the incident and the rather casual approach of the police and I decided to do something about it. I called the police back and told them, "I think I should let you know that I am working on a project for MoD and that I may have had some classified information in the car for which I need to report the incident to MoD Security (ModSy)." MoD's security was highly respected and feared by all government departments including the police. Soon after, I got a phone call from a detective constable that he had been informed of the incident and he wanted to know when he could come and speak with me. It happened to be late Friday evening and he suggested if he could come the next morning and we met early on Saturday morning. He asked me about the project and the kind of information I may have had which I was unable to divulge to him except saying that it may include list of all MoD's locations in the country. He assured me that action would be taken immediately on the incident and they would also inform ModSy. Within 24 hours, I got a phone call from the Metropolitan Police informing me that they had located my car and if a constable could come and pick the spare keys for it. Unfortunately when the officers had come to pick the keys from me, they had left my stolen car in front of the shop where they had spotted it and when they went back to the spot, it was gone. They informed me about this when they came to return the keys a few hours later. Anyway, just over a day later I got another phone call from police saying that they have found my car. Before I could say anything, the officer said, "Don't worry sir, this time we have the car in our possession." After the finger print and other checks were completed and no tempering of the car had been found, it was returned to me. Incidentally, someone happened to find my wallet also thrown in a dustbin. From the ID in the wallet, the person managed to drop it through the letterbox, without the money and credit cards of course.

A few months after the above incident, my company car was due for renewal. I talked to the relevant team in ICL and was told about my options. During the conversation, I also came to know that a new Mercedes had been returned to the pool since the director for whom it was ordered had just left the company. I spoke about it to our commercial manager on the project, who I was quite friendly with. He suggested that although it did not fall within my grade, he might be able to authorise it as it was already in the company pool. One fine week when our CS Project Director was on leave, the commercial manager sent the authorisation of the allocation of the car to me. I was absolutely delighted when I saw the car. It was a Mercedes 190E in metallic cherry red with beige interior. When I reached home with the car, Veena was thrilled to see it and jumped up and gave me a hug. Having a Mercedes as a company car was quite a thing in those days and we thoroughly enjoyed it.

The project started successful roll out to the sites across the country and met all the prescribed targets. I was again involved in visiting the sites prior to their roll out to ensure the site was completely ready. One key roll out event was the MoD Main Building in London. With all the top brass of MoD and defence personnel based in this building, there were very strict requirements that we had to meet with. Installation of terminals to some of these offices had to be done on an appointment basis to ensure that the person was not in his room. The engineer would be met by a security personnel and accompanied to the office. The officer would stay with the engineer till he finished his work and then see him out of the area. Additionally, in order to avoid any tempering with the secure equipment, we were required to hold a stock of 50+ new terminals on the site and the engineer would be given a terminal at random to do the installation in one of the rooms.

Operations Manager at Sainsbury's:

After over a year of successful roll out, I decided to look for another challenge and came across an opportunity to work as CS Operations Manager for Sainsbury's. This was one of the plum jobs in Customer Services with complete responsibility of ICL's service delivery to Sainsbury's Corporate Systems as well as all their stores and petrol stations around the country. It also included managing the subcontractors. From my previous experience there, I had liked their style of management and was delighted to accept the offer. Sainsbury's were a high value client for ICL and their director had a direct link to our CS Director for escalation of any issues. One of the things the General Manager said to me at the time of my appointment was that if I could keep the Sainsbury's Operations Director from escalating any incidents to him, it would make him a very happy man.

We had a small team of engineers based at the headquarter building of Sainsbury's who would provide support to the mainframe systems. My first meeting was with Sainsbury's Operations Director and after a general chat I mentioned to him that if there were any issues I would like him to give me an opportunity to resolve them before escalating them further. He seemed quite happy with this arrangement. In fact, at the end of our meeting he suggested that I also meet their Board Director and set up a meeting with him.

Although our service there was quite satisfactory, I still wanted to make a noticeable improvement in it. At our next meeting with all the sub-contractors, which were Avery, who provided service on the scales in the stores, Symbol who provided support on hand-held scanners and PFS who provided support to petrol stations, I asked them to think of ideas for putting a Continuous Improvement Programme (CIP) in place. For this, we needed the data of performance of each store, which was available in our service desk system. I requested them to provide me the data of the past six months and started analysing it for patterns and trends. Very soon the team got together and identified the areas that had scope for improvements and discussed them with the team at Sainsbury's. Key personnel were identified both from our team as well as from Sainsbury's team as lead persons for each CIP. Very soon we were able to notice improvements in our service that were presented to the customer at our regular management meetings with them. I developed detailed graphical performance reports for these meetings that were so liked by the Operations Director that he wanted to include his Board Director in the distribution list.

Christmas at Sainsbury's:

Every year, Sainsbury's would demand a much higher level of service for the few weeks leading up to and including Christmas. In the past we had to employ additional staff to deliver this service. As Christmas started approaching, I asked our team if we could do something different to enhance our service during this crucial period. Since we now had very accurate data on performance of each store in the country, one suggestion that came up was to carry out preventive maintenance in advance on the worse performing stores. This would mean extra costs on ICL and our partners but I saw benefits in this and discussed the proposal with ICL's Sales Manager and subsequently with Sainsbury's Operations Director.

They liked the proposal and even agreed to share the costs with us on the condition that we agree to deliver service of a much higher level. We were also offered an incentive of a bonus on meeting this enhanced service target. We were confident of our approach and signed the agreement. I presented our plan to the Customer Service Managers around the country and got their buy in. The only measure of success of this project that I can give you is that we received the bonus as well as a statement from their Board Director stating, "This is the best service we have ever received from ICL."

My next role was as the commercial manager for South East Retail Services Division followed by Development Manager for ICL's Post Office system Horizon. . This required a considerable amount of travelling again. After a while, I started to think of doing something different, perhaps something of my own and decided to leave ICL.

I found ICL to be a highly professionally run organisation that provided good career opportunities to all its employees and duly rewarded them for their effort and achievements.

After ICL:

I got together with a friend of mine who had considerable experience as a travel agent and we decided to start a travel agency. We set up the company and hired the premises. Unfortunately, my friend got serious health issues and had to discontinue. He asked me to continue on my own hoping that he would perhaps be able to join me in six month's time. Having had no experience in business and no knowledge of travel agency business in particular, I decided to abandon the idea.

In order to keep my national insurance contributions up to date, I had to register at the Social Security office. I was interviewed by a manager at regular intervals to ensure that I was seeking employment in earnest and also assist me to find a job. On one of my interview dates, I was told the manager was not there and was asked to come the following week. When I turned up there the following week and was told the same thing, I got irritated and said to them, "Just because we do not have a job doesn't mean you can treat us like this. Why could you not inform me that the manager was not in and I should not bother coming?" Hearing the commotion going on at the front desk, one of the senior managers came out and took me to her room. She inquired about my background and asked me if I was interested in a job with DHSS as they had recently launched a new project. After due formalities I was made an offer of a job as an Action Team Advisor.

I worked in the project for just over a year and decided to look for something else. This is when I landed with Ascham Homes, an Arms Length Management Organisation (ALMO) of London Borough of Waltham Forest and finally retired from there as the Head of Information Technology.

A friendly advice to youngsters:

From my experience of having come from India to build a career in the UK, I would suggest to any youngsters following this path to not draw any barriers around them or limit themselves by imaginary 'glass ceiling'. Although I did not push myself for promotions in ICL but having got to the next level I never found myself lacking in any way in my peer group. And yes, the promotions came my way in plenty reaching the Senior Management level in the company.

5. Yoga – the passion

My first brush with yoga was when I was around 10 years old and we were living on Irwin Road. In summer we would pull our cots out and sleep in the veranda at the front of the house. A friend of my father used to drive to our house to pick up my father to go to the yoga ashram on Aravalli hills behind *Birla Mandir*. During the summer holidays, my father would wake me up also at 5:30 am to accompany him to the yoga class. I would sometimes escape using some excuse but otherwise had to go with him. For a boy of my age yoga was not an interesting activity. The only pleasure I got was to see some of the older people toppling all over the place while attempting to do the balancing postures.

Teachers Diploma in 1999:

After a few years in UK my interest in yoga was re-ignited and I started going to weekly yoga class held at Gearies School in Ilford. I quite enjoyed the class and continued for a few years, which developed an inspiration in me to take up teaching of yoga.

As I was still in full time employment, I joined a two years diploma course of British Wheel of Yoga (BWY) where the classes were scheduled for Sundays. The class turned out to be a very good mix of 3 boys and 9 girls of different ages and abilities. We all bonded very well and enjoyed our full day Sunday sessions. Our teacher had an experience of many years of yoga practice. She had drawn up an excellent curriculum covering the background and philosophy of yoga, introduction of Bhagvad Gita and Upnishads, and detailed practice and benefits of the asanas and some pranayams. She also covered human anatomy to help us have a good understanding of our body. The course ended with us conducting a full yoga class, which was inspected and assessed by invigilators. I completed my course and obtained the diploma in June 1999. Thereafter, I started taking classes at the local gym and also carried on with my own practice at home.

Swami Ramdev's visit to UK:

In 2006, Swami Ramdev was to come to UK to hold a *shivir* (camp) in Ilford. I saw an opportunity here to use my connection with BWY and spread his teachings and message in UK. I sought a meeting with the organisers to discuss about interviewing Swami Ramdev and publish it in the BWY magazine. I took Gill Pendreich with me, who was a part of the team responsible for education in BWY. The organisers were rather pleased with our proposal and gave both of us a VVIP pass for the whole week of the shivir.

During the shivir we interviewed Baba Ramdev and asked him about the great emphasis he placed on pranayams in his teaching. He explained that although the asanas had a very good effect on the muscles and joints of the body, the pranayams had a much greater influence on the internal organs. I continued to attend the camp every day, sometimes with my wife. One day my sister accompanied me and was absolutely delighted to see that we were seated right in the front row. Finally, we published a two-page article of the interview with Baba Ramdev in the BWY magazine.

After my retirement I stopped taking the classes and focussed instead on developing my own practice. I wanted to develop something that was simple yet effective and could be performed by people of all ages and abilities. The practice focused on the following aspects.

• asanas to build suppleness and strength in the muscles
• pranayams to enhance and maintain the functioning of internal organs
• limbering exercises to improve flexibility and mobility of all the joints
• bring in the traditional approach of 'focussed breathing' to relax the muscles which are stretched during the asanas

This resulted in me publishing a book on yoga "Develop Health and Inner Peace Through Meditational Yoga" that was released in 2018.

In November 2014 Prime Minister Modi got the United Nations Assembly to declare 21 June as the International Day of Yoga (IDY). The HCI in UK set up a meeting to plan for the event on June 2015. I was invited to this meeting, which was chaired by the High Commissioner Mr Mathai. A number of yoga organisations were also present and put forward their plans for the celebration of the day. I made a suggestion that it would perhaps be a good idea to kick off the event by holding a yoga session at the High Commission and invite some dignitaries to it. The idea appealed to Mr Mathai and a yoga session was included as the opening activity for the day's events. The Sivananda Yoga group conducted the session and I with some other people from the planning team participated in the same. A number of MPs, Lords and other dignitaries were invited and the day turned out to be a huge success. The HCI received uplifting commendations from the Indian government on their enthusiastic promotion of the event.

Every year since then I have been a part of the planning meetings at the HCI in UK. For the celebration of International Day of Yoga in 2016, I joined the boat trip on river Thames organised by Sivananda Yoga Centre. A large group of people took part in the yoga practice on the boat and a big banner was hung outside publicising the IDY. Now the International Day of Yoga is being celebrated throughout the world every year with a lot of interest and enthusiasm.

Book Launch in 2018

Before I write about my book, I would like to explain what I mean by meditational yoga.

- First thing I do when I begin the yoga practice is to take my body into a state of meditation by using full yoga breath with focussed breathing and visualisation
- This meditative state creates an environment for the body to provide constant feedback and act as a guide during the course of the practice.

This approach allows me to multiply the benefits of the yoga practice many fold. Using it, I have been able to develop peace of mind and shed the unnecessary baggage from my mind.

My book was launched jointly by the High Commissioner and Swami Ramdev during the IDY celebrations at the High Commission in June 2018.

Conducting a Yoga Class at IDY 2019:

I had the honour with an opportunity to hold a yoga class at the High Commission of India in 2019 to kick off the International Day of Yoga event. The class was held in the Mahatma Gandhi Hall and over 50 people attended it including a number of High Commission's staff.

6. Jain Association

Jain Association of UK was formed in 1977 and one of its founder members Mrs Pushpa Kalraiya set up a simple temple at her home. We joined the association soon after but lost contact with it after a few years. At the time of my father's first visit in the summer of 1987, Mr P R Jain, who lived near us in Seven Kings, was the president of the Association. In an effort to revive the membership of the organisation, he picked up our name from the local telephone directory and called on us one evening. I introduced him to our family including my father. He and my father were talking for a few minutes and soon they found common contacts back home in Haryana and were talking as if they had known each other for years. This is something I always admired in their generation that they had such an awareness of the wider families of their circle of friends and could easily find connections through long linked relations.

We had a good chat and I agreed to actively participate in the Association. We attended the next monthly meeting held at Mrs Kalraiya's residence. We met with some of the members from before and got introduced to some of the new members. We found a nice welcome and started attending the meetings on a regular basis. Veena and I are both very social and find it easy to make friends. Soon we became actively involved in the work of the association and I was elected to the Executive Committee and given the office of General Secretary.

The association used to hold a monthly gathering either at the above temple or at the residence of one of the members whenever someone offered to do so. In addition the Association used to hold two major celebrations in the year namely

- Mahavir Jayanti to celebrate the birth of lord Mahavir and
- Diwali to celebrate the attainment of nirvana by lord Mahavir

We also celebrated *Paryushan* and *Das Lakshan parva*, which were usually held at the temple.

Mahavir Jayanti was very much a religious festival with some speeches on Jain religion and associated topics, some bhajans and ending with a good vegetarian meal. It was free to all members and wider community to attend. Diwali, however, was more of a joyful event with some religious flair but also lot of entertainment and fun with music and dance and finally ending with a delicious meal.

I wanted to make the next Mahavir Jayanti function a bit more interesting and entertaining, while still retaining its religious character, in order that non-jains could also enjoy the function. For this we included a few dances and professional bhajan singers in addition to the usual programme. I also invited the High Commissioner of India as the chief guest. We had agreed at the EC meeting that we could also invite our non-jain friends to the event. The function was held at the iconic Bhartiya Vidya Bhavan in Hammersmith and was a huge success with over 300 seating hall filled to capacity with people flocking in the isles. These celebrations became a popular event in the Associations calendar with the High Commissioner or similar dignitaries as the chief guest. I remember one interesting incident at one of these celebrations. At this function, the High Commissioner Dr Singhvi asked me, "Should I give my address in Hindi or English" and I told him that most members would be comfortable in either. He decided to make his speech in perfect Hindi language as he had very good command of both languages. In my vote of thanks I made a comment on this saying "Dr Singhvi asked me about making his address in Hindi or English but this has now put me in an embarrassing situation to respond as my Hindi is not as good". Anyway I made my speech in a mixture of Hindi and English.

We also made some changes to the next Diwali function by again adding some quality dances, singers and music to dance to. We invited the first secretary of High Commission as chief guest at this event. The function was held at the Indian YMCA and was again thoroughly enjoyed by a good crowd of our members.

Success of these events got the association in a more active mood and greater number of members started attending the monthly meetings. After a couple of years I was elected to the post of President and carried this role for four years. The High Commissioner became a regular chief guest at our Mahavir Jayanti functions and I developed a good personal relationship with him. I was included in the list of invitees to the functions held at the High Commission and also had the pleasure of attending a number of gatherings and garden parties at the High Commissioner's residence. One of our close friends asked us if they could join us to attend one of these functions. After getting the agreement from the High Commissioner's office we took them along. On reaching the residence we were met by the High

Commissioner at the entrance and as I apologised to him for being a bit late, he jokingly remarked, "No problem Jiwan ji, we were just waiting for you to start the function". Our friends were totally bowled over by his friendliness towards us. The function was in celebration of Buddha Jayanti and happened to have some high level dignitaries including the Services Chiefs and Justice of Supreme Court from India, who, our friend who was a lawyer could not have been more delighted to meet with.

I had become aware of as many as 28 Jain organisations in UK and felt that there should be an opportunity for us all to work together. With this in mind we started inviting heads of these organisations to our functions and many of them did attend. It was at this time that an initiative was taken by the Institute Of Jainology (IOJ) to form an umbrella group to bring all the Jain organisations under one banner. As President of our Association I became actively involved in the working party.

In November 2010, Institute of Jainology organised an exhibition to launch Jainpedia, a collection of Jain manuscripts and art, at the Victoria and Albert museum and invited Prince Charles as chief guest. I had the opportunity to meet with Prince Charles at the launch ceremony and have a brief chat with him about Jain Association.

In November 2012 IOJ organised a meeting at the Vatican and I was invited to be a part of this Jain delegation. We had a very fruitful meeting that was chaired by Jean Louis Cardinal Tauran, President of the Pontifical Council for Interfaith Dialogue. After the morning meeting we took the members of the Vatican for lunch at a pure vegetarian Indian restaurant.

The atmosphere at lunch was very cordial and light hearted and I managed to throw in a little joke. 'Once the pope decided that he wanted to drive the car. As they got out of the city limits he asked the driver to stop the car and move to the back seat and let him drive the car. He quite enjoyed the drive and was soon running over the speed limit on the motorway. A police car intercepted them and asked the driver to stop and lower the window. As soon as the policeman saw the pope, he panicked and ran to contact his superior on the phone asking him to come over. When the superior asked what the matter was and book whoever it is. He said "sir I can't, it is pope himself who is driving the car, can you imagine who will be in back". They seemed to enjoy the joke and one person said; "sure, we will not tell the pope about this".

In the afternoon we were given an escorted tour of the Vatican including their private library that houses the earliest original copy of the Bible.

Nitin Mehta's Vegetarian rally:

Nitin Mehta is a close friend of mine and runs the Vegetarian Society in the UK. He would also be an invitee to our Mahavir Jayanti programmes and would sometimes be asked to give a brief speech. Once he held a large rally in the ground of Alexandra Palace to promote vegetarianism and had some key dignitaries there including the heads of some of the Jain Organisations. At one point he invited all the heads of the organisations and other dignitaries to the stage to take an oath of vegetarianism and to promote the same. I happened to be a part of this group and took this oath. As I had strayed from the path earlier, I said to Veena on our way back home, "it feels strange that on one side I am taking this oath on the stage but I know that I am not following it. I am going to change and become completely vegetarian again". And I have held to that promise ever since.

7. Lifetime of Holidays

"Love of the family and friends is life's greatest blessing"

VISIT TO JAIN PLACES OF WORSHIP (*Tiraths*)

My leaning towards the Jain places of worship has been predominantly towards three: Shri Mahavir Ji, Gomateshwara Temple and Ranakpur Temple.

Shri Mahavir Ji: My fascination for Shri Mahavir Ji may be because of its proximity to Delhi and also due to it being the place my father visited frequently, either on his own or with family. It is also the first religious place Veena and I visited soon after our marriage. After which we have made many trips to the temple on our visits to India.

Gomateshwara Temple: It has a 57 feet high granite monolith of Lord Bahubali, son of Lord Rishabhnath who was the first *tirthankara* of Jains. It is built at the top of a hill in Shravanabelgola. The experience we have had on our visits here has made this a favourite of mine.

We arranged a visit here to perform a *pooja* (a ceremonial prayer) at the statue of Lord Bahubali. Using my uncle's influence, we had booked accommodation at Sahu Jain's bungalow just next to the hill where the statue is. As we arrived late in the evening, the priest of the temple advised us to have dinner and attend the evening arti at the temple. We thoroughly enjoyed the arti and went to sleep. We were to go to the top of the hill early next morning for the pooja ceremony.

We reached the temple in the morning and I was asked to have a bath and change into a *dhoti*. The *pujari* (priest) performed the pooja after drawing a cordon around the area to prevent people from entering there. The place draws several tourists and worshippers every day. Many tourists were sitting down in the yard in front observing the ceremony in silence. I felt very humbled to be in the area where the pooja was being performed. It was a great honour and I was delighted for having performed the ceremony and came back with a very happy feeling from the visit.

We had hired a car for the entire duration of our trip and made our way back to Bangalore. On the way, Veena mentioned that as we were not too far from Tirupati Balaji, will we be able to visit it. I asked the driver, who was himself a devotee and a regular visitor to the temple about the possibility. He said, "Sir, it is about 10 hours drive. But if you are keen, I would be happy to take you there."

All greed and we made our way to Tirupati, one of the most revered temples of South India. We arrived there just after 9 pm and started to look for accommodation for the night. After enquiring at a few places in vain, we were told that there may be a chance at the newly opened residence of one of the sects. There was a room available there but the manager refused saying it was only for the members of the sect. We managed to persuade him saying that we needed it only for a few hours and none of their members was likely to come in so late at night. This sorted, our attention got shifted to the urgency of getting the entry tickets for the temple for next morning. We dashed to the ticket office only to find that they had closed for the day. However, we were told that there were no tickets available and only the management could authorise some.

Things were not looking too bright. There are three early morning sessions starting at 0330 with limited number of tickets which are booked much in advance, sometimes even years earlier. I realized I will need all my charm and will have to use my best persuasive skills to get a result. I approached the management office and explained our situation saying that we had come all the way from UK for this visit and had to catch our flight back early next morning. To my absolute delight and amazement, I was able to persuade the manager. He agreed to grant us the tickets. In fact, he gave us the ticket for the '*Suprabhatam Seva*' that is considered the ultimate experience. Knowing his interest, I also bought a ticket for the driver. However, he declined saying, "Sir, since it's a long drive to the airport next morning, it is better for me to have some rest in the night".

We only realized the significance of our tickets when we met the other members in the group who had booked for them more than a year in advance. It was a 'darshan' or *seva* matching everything that has been written about it.

These two temple visits have left an everlasting impression on our minds.

Ranakpur Temple: The thing that impresses me most about this place is its magnificent design and architecture, equalling the best in the whole country. My first visit to Ranakpur temple was long time ago when it had not been developed into a tourist attraction. I drove there from Udaipur and could see this monumental structure suddenly rise in front of my eyes as we went over the hump of the hill. The beauty of the interior of the temple left me as much in awe as did its external architecture. On a further tour of India, I was fortunate enough to visit this place again along with Veena.

Sammed Shikhar ji is one of the most revered places for Jains as 20 of our *tirthankars* achieved *nirvana* (salvation) from here. There is a commonly held belief about the sanctity of this place that if you make a complete round trip of the 20 hill tops, you will escape going to hell or be reborn in the form of a dog. On one of our visits to India, we decided to take this journey, It was quite an arduous trip but we managed to complete the trek satisfactorily putting our mind to rest about our re-birth.

Los Angeles, California and Las Vegas – Jun' 1997:

We planned a visit to Los Angeles and decided to stay with my childhood friend Vinod's family. As we were going to travel around, I had booked a package that included hire of a car for the duration of our stay. Vinod came to pick us up at the airport and suggested that Geeta drove our hired car rather than me taking the reins of it straight away. Gradually, I was able to drive around without any trouble. Very kindly, Vinod showed us around Los Angeles giving us a wonderful time. Early on in our trip I decided to buy a Canon 514 XLS camcorder to be able to capture the memories of our holidays.

For our visit to California, we had booked and paid for a hotel in advance. As per our plan, we were to follow route A1 which is a rather scenic route running alongside Pacific coastline most of the way. However, Vinod suggested a stopover at Madonna's hotel enroute, which is a rather colourful place with everything in pink and a delicious meal on offer.

When we arrived at our hotel in California, the lobby seemed rather full and we were told that they had no booking for us. I spoke to Vinod who confirmed that we did make a booking. We decided to look for another hotel and found one not so far away. When we reached the new hotel, we were told the possible reason for our missing booking in the earlier hotel. There was a gay parade scheduled in California next day and the earlier hotel was a usual haunt for this group. After completing our sightseeing, we headed towards Las Vegas and were advised to go via Yosemite Park. It is a large and beautiful park with a variety of scenery including falling 'burning logs' from the side of the mountain.

On our way to Las Vegas, we had to pass through the Death Valley with miles of desert. We stopped at a motel on the way and in the vegetarian offering the waiter suggested 'potato and pea soup' which we thought was an odd combination. But he insisted saying that it was one of their most popular recipes. I decided to give it a try and to my surprise enjoyed it tremendously.

We reached our hotel in Las Vegas and were joined by Vinod who had also come straight there. While going to our room from the underground car parking, we had to pass through the Casino. I was amazed to see its size and decided to come back to it. After settling the family in our room, I went back to the casino saying I had left something in the car. I played on one of the 'one-arm-bandits' and was doing pretty well when I spotted Vinod also walk into the casino. My machine was doing good and very soon I was up by over $100. I decided to end the session marking its location in my mind to come back to it the next day. However, when we came to the casino the next day, the size of the hall and the large number of machines did not allow me to locate my marked machine.

The next morning, we went to Ceaser Hotel for breakfast on Vinod's suggestion. The size of the dining hall and the range of food there was absolutely amazing and the whole buffet was for a fixed price of $1.99. We filled our plates to sample as many items as we could and thoroughly enjoyed the breakfast. We went to explore the other hotels and also the displays and shows that were running there. It was all mind boggling with each hotel trying to outdo the others in their decor and shows. We also enjoyed the magnificent fountain display with lights and sound outside the Ceaser's Palace.

A visit to the amusement park, Disneyland was everything that we had heard about it and more. There were fantastic rides and entertainment for the whole family, some of the key ones being the roller coaster ride for the brave-hearted, and the Ferris wheel.

There was live entertainment throughout the park with many Disney characters like Winnie-the-Pooh, Goofie and Mickey & Minnie Mouse greeting the visitors, interacting with children, and posing for photos. The Disneyland Band is also a part of the entertainment in the park.

Another prominent feature was the parades including the Main Street Electric Parade and Parade of Dreams with famous Disneyland characters from films. There were also a large number of floats that formed a part of these parades

On our visit to the Universal Studios, we had the opportunity to see the sets of some of the iconic Hollywood movies. On one such set, we were going through a large hangar. It seemed there was nothing much to see there. Suddenly, we heard the sound of a train approaching and a runaway train appeared from our left. Before we could catch our wits, the train approached us at a great speed and appeared to come straight to hit us. Everyone jumped and started to run away only to find that the train had come to a sudden halt. This was a replica of a scene from one of the movies and we realised how these scenes appear so real on the screen.

Cornwall – Jun' 1997:

Cornwall in the south west of England, dubbed as English Riviera, is a popular tourist destination with beautiful coastline, beaches and picturesque harbour villages. We decided to explore this area with Puran Chand ji and Jiji during their visit to UK. A lovely chalet style bungalow in a resort was to be our base for the week. St Ives with its beautiful beaches is one of the scenic and quintessential British villages in Cornwall. We decided to have lunch at a hotel perched atop a hill with views of the beach and the sea. Land's End, which marks the southwest tip of England, was another port of call for us. Another popular destination around the area is Newquay beach and we were fortunate and pleased to witness a surfing competition taking place there on the day we visited it. Apart from these, there were a lot of other activities on offer at the resort and a number of good drives around the bay area and countryside filled the rest of our week.

Mediterranean cruise – 1999:

Our first cruise holiday was to the Mediterranean in 1999. We flew into Majorca and boarded the ship named Island Breeze from there. On the first evening, there was a programme arranged by the crew in the auditorium to tell everyone about the schedule of activities on the ship. They announced that the next evening would be dinner with the captain followed by a Family Fortune programme in the auditorium. In my excitement, I went to the presenter and asked if they were going to look for participants for the Family Fortune show from amongst the travellers. On finding that we were a family of four, he would not let me move from there till I had completed the form to enter. The family did not take this very kindly but everyone went along in the spirit of the holiday.

Next evening, all of us dressed up for the evening with Veena in a beautiful blue saree, me wearing my Nehru suit and Maneesh and Sasha in their suitable outfits. We had our dinner, met the captain and made our way to the hall. The presenter came and asked us to wait in the front row to be called on stage. The hall was not too crowded initially which gave us some comfort. Soon the programme started and the presenter introduced us and invited us on the stage. He had also managed to find another family of four and introduced and invited them on the stage as well. We noticed that the hall was getting full very fast as people were making way to it after having dinner. We played the game and won it. We were presented with a bottle of champagne and a T-shirt each with the logo of the ship on one side and number 1 printed on the other side. Another outcome of this was that most of the people on the ship came to know our names and would say hello to us or have a brief chat whenever we met. Sasha also became a little celebrity on the ship.

I decided to wear my Tee shirt on the ship but others were not all keen to wear the same. I happened to meet the presenter of the programme in the passing and he said it was nice that I was wearing the shirt. But when I told him the rest of the family is not so keen on it, he suggested he would replace their tee shirts with a bottle of champagne instead, which he did. Every evening when we went for dinner we will carry our bottle with us. When asked the waiter for a bucket for the bottle, he brought a bucket with a chilled bottle in it and replaced our bottle with that. And this would go on for another few nights.

Apart from this we enjoyed the cruise tremendously for the freedom it gave us in travelling from place to place and not having to pack and unpack every time. The food on the ship had a huge variety and we had a good selection of vegetarian meals. There were a lot of activities that we could take part including a number of shows in the evenings.

Since then cruising has become our favourite form of holiday.

Cruise on River Nile and Cairo –Nov' 2001

We booked an all-inclusive 5-star Cruise on River Nile with a specialist company called Voyages Jules Verne. The tour consisted of 4 days on river Nile and 4 days in Cairo. We boarded our boat at Luxor and visited the main attractions of Luxor Temple, Valley of the Kings (Tutankhamen), Valley of the Queens, Karnak Temple Hatshepsut, Khnum Temples, Collossi of Memnon and Kom Obo Temple. The architecture and scale of some of these structures left us spellbound.

There was extensive entertainment on the boat including a belly dancer and a day of fancy dress party when we all dressed in the traditional Egyptian costumes. There were about 25 people on our boat with us. We were the only Indian family but the whole group bonded really well. We moved on to Aswan Dam and then to take a felucca ride. On the boat, the staff played traditional Egyptian music, which had a very nice tempo to it, and everyone danced to its rhythm. After a while we heard the sound of 'she'll be coming round the mountain when she comes' in the distance. Soon we could see a small rowing boat with a group of little kids approaching us. They started singing louder as they came closer to our boat. The guide advised us to just give them some simple things if we wished to and we did.

We proceeded on our way to Cairo, where we stayed at the Hilton Hotel. Since we had been missing a proper Indian meal, we headed to Mina House Oberoi hotel at the top of Cairo Road, as recommended by our tour guide. No sooner had we been seated at the table, a group of musicians came and occupied the stage that was right in front of us. They started playing *bollywood* songs and seeing our interest they called the manager and said something to him. The manager came to our table and said if we had a request the musicians would be happy to play it for us. We took some time and wrote down a few of our favourite numbers. To our utmost delight, the musicians started playing these very songs for us. We thoroughly enjoyed the songs with the delicious meal we had ordered.

Next morning at breakfast, others asked us where we had disappeared for dinner. When we told them about the Indian meal and how nice it was, some of them said they would have accompanied us if they had known about it. Eventually it was agreed that we should make another trip to the hotel the next day. We went there as planned and were gradually joined by 20 other travellers on our boat. They told the manager that he should thank us, as we were the ones who had brought them all there. As a gesture, the manager made our meal complementary and did not charge us for it. Some of our companions loved the place and claimed it was the best Indian meal they had ever had.

During daytime, we went to visit the museum, pyramids and markets. I was amazed to see the intricate gold jewellery on display in the museum and have always wondered how the craftsman could make such delicate pieces without the technology that we have today. While going around the markets we were approached by some children shouting 'Amitabh Bachchan', 'Shah Rukh Khan'. They held on to my finger and walked along with us may be with the hope that we will take them to meet the two actors. In the evening, we went to see the sound and light show at the Sphinx.

Switzerland – 2001:

The picturesque town of Engelberg was chosen for our visit to Switzerland. The families of both Veena's sisters who had flown in straight from India joined us. We were all staying at the Ramada Hotel right in the heart of the town.

A gently sloping mountainous terrain, lush greenery and chalet style Swiss houses with flower boxes in the windows presented the nature's beauty at its best. This could only find a parallel with snow-covered mountaintops of Titlis and Jungfrau. A trip to the top of Titlis Mountain in a gondola was our first experience of the cable car. Specially designed train bogeys with large glass windows and a glass roof made the visit to Jungfrau a very scenic one. The town seemed to be a popular destination for Indian tourists and signs in Hindi were commonly seen everywhere.

On our usual evening stroll along the high street one evening, we found a large number of families with children in their colourful attire lining up on the street on both sides. On enquiring we found that it was Switzerland's national day, which most towns celebrated in their own way. Soon a procession started to appear from the monastery end of the high street with many people carrying the Chinese lanterns in red colour, the same as on the Swiss national flag. More people on the street started buying the lanterns and joined the procession and we also followed suit. The procession led by the band reached the town square, just opposite our hotel. The band included the Alphorn (alpine horn), which was a delight for us to hear.

It was a nice sunny morning next day and as I looked out of our bedroom window I saw a number of hang-gliders floating in the air with the backdrop of snow-covered Alps. It was such a delightful sight and something that had always attracted me that I went and booked a flight for myself for the next day. I was advised to call them an hour before my flight time to confirm as sometimes they had to cancel the flight depending on the weather conditions.

Unfortunately, this is what happened the next morning and my flight was cancelled. Perhaps something for my tick-list for our next visit.

Prague – Sep' 2005:

This was a long weekend break that we took with two other couples Goels and Agrawals.

Like most European cities, Prague has a town square that was the meeting place for locals and a key attraction for the tourists. One of the attractions in the square was the horse drawn carriage that will take you around the town in an elegant style. Czechoslovakia is renowned for its cut glass crystal ware and we took the opportunity to buy a set of whiskey glasses.

The State Opera House was an impressive looking building and we decided to book an evening's performance there. As the performance started we felt totally at a loss – 'English speaking tourists, watching an opera in Czechoslovakia, which was being played in Italian'. I decided to get hold of a program in English and read the story, which was about a priest and a young woman. We were then able to follow the story and enjoy the performance.

A cruise on the river and a tour of the city were some other attractions.

Mahamastakabhishek – Feb' 2006

As I mentioned earlier Gomateshwara Temple has always been one of my most revered religious places. So, when the opportunity arose in 2006 to take part in the *mahamastakabhishek* celebrations, I decided to travel to

Bangalore from UK. The ceremony is held once every 12 years anointing the statue of Lord Bahubali with seven elements namely water, milk, saffron, sandalwood paste, rice flour, sugarcane juice and flowers. A huge multi-storeyed structure is built around the statue to provide platform for people to sit and also for anointing to take place from the top of the head. Lakhs of people from all around the world come to visit these celebrations.

Individuals who wish to carry out the anointment using each of above items are selected by a bidding process (known as *boli*) and the highest bidder for each has the honour to perform the ceremony. On the day we were visiting, most of the bids had gone and the next bid was for the flowers. As the bidding started, I jokingly said to my cousin that he should go for the bid and he reverted by saying, "Jiwan you are the rich man coming from London. You should be the one to bid". When I told him that I was interested but did not wish to go that high, he signalled to one of the organisers to come. My cousin knew the organiser, who also came from Daryaganj. When my cousin told him that I was interested in making a bid but could not go that high, the gentlemen asked me how high could I go and I told him my limit. He went back and returned soon to say that the bid was mine and the announcement was soon made with my name as the winner of the bid for the flower anointment. This was something that I could not have imagined in my wildest dream when I was coming for the ceremony from UK.

We were asked to go to the topmost platform when our turn came. My cousin accompanied me and as we were going up he invited a few others saying, "Come along, my brother is doing the ceremony". Soon we had a good group of around 20-25 people on the platform and it was the most exhilarating experience to be where we were.

When I was returning to Delhi, one couple came to me at the airport and said, "Thank you Jiwan ji, it was like a dream for us to be able to do that ceremony because of you". I did not know the gentleman but he must have been one of my cousin's friends who participated with us.

Cruise on QE2 – Oct' 2007:

A cruise on the QE2 was considered a benchmark in luxury and we decided to sample this with a three-day trip to Europe. I must admit we were not that impressed by the ship. Perhaps it was a status symbol till the new and modern ships had not appeared on the scene. Anyhow, our journey was quite pleasant with a visit to Bruges with its canals, cobbled streets and medieval buildings.

China – Dec' 2007:

To celebrate Veena's 60th birthday, our children booked a holiday for us to China. Our first port of call was Shanghai where we were booked in a suite on the tenth floor of Hotel Shangri-La, overlooking the Huangpu River. Opposite the hotel across the river was the Bund, a promenade that was a well-known tourist attraction. Shanghai had the most luxurious and artistic looking airport and was equally matched by the roads leading out of it.

On a sightseeing visit to Pudong, we were escorted by some school girls who wanted to accompany us. On being asked why they wanted to be with us, they said excitedly, "We want to practice our English speaking with you". They also started telling us about the town and in particular about tea tasting and eventually took us to one of the centres. This place followed a very lengthy but delicate procedure of preparing tea including adding some magic flowers that come into full bloom as you pour hot water on them. The girls did not participate in the ceremony but waited outside for us.

There was a lot to see in Shanghai including the shopping centres, splendid Yu Gardens and some Chinese historical places. There was a huge underground shopping centre running under the hotel and spread over a vast area. During our visit to the Yu Gardens, we met an Indian family and asked them if they knew of some good Indian places to eat. The gentleman worked for a large Indian corporate and was a regular visitor to Shanghai. He recommended a restaurant in one of the big hotels. Surprisingly, they served a good selection of vegetarian meal, which was pretty delicious considering we were in China.

The front desk had informed us of the swimming pool in the basement but we were not too keen to use it knowing what the basement pools look and feel like. However, we decided to just go and see it and were absolutely gobsmacked seeing the beauty of the pool. It was quite a large pool set up like a grotto with greenery and flowers at one end, beautiful scenery on some of the walls and lighting to make it into a really attractive place. We did enjoy our swim in it after all!

We were also keen to taste a typical Chinese vegetarian meal and enquired at the hotel desk for their recommendation. The manager suggested a place called 'Pure Lotus' and due to its remote location suggested that we take a cab there. At the same time, he called for a cab and relayed some instructions to the driver in Chinese making a note of the cab's number. When we reached the restaurant there was a considerable queue there and we had to wait for around 15-20 minutes. Finally, we were seated in a room that was like their family room and were served our meal there. The meal was really delicious and we were glad we decided to go there. When we wanted to go back to the hotel, we asked the restaurant to arrange for a cab. Like our hotel manager, they also called a cab, relayed instruction to the driver in Chinese and made a note of his cab's number. We reached our hotel safely wondering about the instructions being passed and the numbers of the cabs being noted. We still don't know whether this was done keeping our safety in mind or was it 'big brother' in China keeping an eye on us.

Our next stop was Beijing where we stayed at the Grand Hyatt hotel, which was not too far from Tiananmen Square and the Palace Museum. The palace museum is spread over a very large area and has some beautiful buildings in typical Chinese style. It is so huge that you can spend a whole day exploring it. The Tiananmen Square (meaning Gate of Heavenly Peace) is a large square in the city centre and can hold over 500000 people. Some of the buildings in the square include Monument to the People's Heroes, Mao Zedong (or Mao TseTung) Mausoleum, Great Hall of the People and the National Museum of China.

In Beijing a visit to the Hongqiao Pearl Market is an absolute must. This four-storey building offers everything from bags, shoes, clothes, silk, tea, tablecloth, toys, souvenirs, pearls to watches and jewelry. It is also the heart of replica of branded goods particularly luggage, watches and the like. I remember visiting a luggage shop and asking them about the make a particular set of bags. We were told very casually, "whatever you want". It was so reasonably priced that we told him to give us Samsonite. He asked us to be back in an hour to collect the bags. We returned after an hour and our three pieces of luggage were marked with proper Samsonite labels. Incidentally, they gave us a pretty good service over a number of years of travel.

Rather than taking a guided tour of the Great Wall of China we were recommended to take a cab from the Hotel to see it. The driver took us to a spot, which gave us a good opportunity to explore the place. All of us decided to walk up on the wall. Veena and I stopped at the point where it had become quite steep to go further while Maneesh and Sasha carried on. They also found it quite tough to maintain their balance while coming downhill on their way back. An adventurous day overall was the verdict.

Mysore and Bangalore in India – Feb' 2008:

We planned a visit to India to attend a couple of weddings in the family and decided to include a trip to the South covering Mysore and Bangalore. We made our base at a hotel in Bangalore and booked a car for the whole trip. Our first visit was to the two famous temples, the Keshva Temple in Belur and Shiva Temple in Halebidu. A few temples in India can only match the exquisite architecture and detailed and intricate sculpting of these temples. Next, we visited the Mysore palace and Brindavan gardens with its beautiful landscape and fountains with a *'son et lumiere'* show.

Singapore and Bali – Jan' 2009

Just after his marriage, Maneesh went on an assignment to Singapore with Dresdner Bank. He had a lovely apartment with a very large balcony overlooking the river. On the other side of the river from his apartment was the central area, which was the heart of the evening life, eating places and entertainment. Singapore happens to be a young and modern country with not much of cultural or architectural history as most of the construction is new. As we came out of the airport, the first thing we noticed was how neat and clean everything was. On the way to Maneesh's apartment the driver told us how popular their Prime Minister was. He was a good visionary and focused on looking after the interest of his people and nation building. One notable thing about the country was its discipline and the way everything ran to order. Maneesh used to get an SMS on his phone 10 minutes before his bus was scheduled to arrive at his bus stop and he would just walk up there to catch it in time.

Maneesh's apartment had a large rooftop eternity pool. It was something I had seen for the first time and it felt exciting as well as a bit strange to swim by the edge of the pool. A few of the attractions in the country included the botanical gardens, Santosa Island and Raffles Hotel. Raffles was an old historic place and still followed the tradition from British days to throw the peanut peels on the bar floor but was otherwise a very neat and clean hotel. There was a unique laser and music show at Santosa Island where the pictures were projected on a vapour like screen of water.

We were to travel to Bali next where Sasha had booked accommodation for us at The Mansion in a tiny village called Ubud. This was perhaps the most majestic and peaceful stay of all our holidays around the world. The Mansion (hotel) was owned by a very rich Korean lady who would visit the place every year for a few weeks. The main building had a huge lobby and a library-cum-study on the ground floor and her living quarters on the first floor. There were large gardens and three cottages, which were the only accommodation for the guests. We were allocated the cottage that had three suites and a shared lobby. Veena and I took the main suite that was an open plan room with a large four-poster bed with chintz curtains and a large sunken bathtub in marble at one side of the room. Two life-size urchins stood by the side of the bathtub and held bowls in their hands through which water was pouring into the tub. There was a screen that obscured the view of the bathtub from the rest of the room. Sasha occupied the other suite in our cottage.

There was another cottage next to ours, which was followed by a gazebo with keep-fit equipment including a treadmill, a cycle and an area to do yoga. The huts at the end of the garden housed the massage rooms. There was a swimming pool on one side of the garden and another one outside the main complex of The Mansion. Opposite our cottage was the restaurant set in a typical Balinese style. Even today, the serenity of the whole place just leaves me without words to be able to describe it.

Bali has rich cultural and architectural heritage that was reflected in its temples dating back to when it was under Hindu rulers. These Hindu temples have a beautiful architecture. Some of them are in pretty good shape while others have turned into ruins. Another thing we noticed around the village was that the shopkeepers were very religious. As soon as you entered a shop you would see an alcove at the side of the entrance with pictures or statues of deities, mostly Hindu. There would also be a *diya* (a small earthenware lamp) lit in the front of the shop in the morning.

The village of Ubud is known for its handicraft and painting markets. One young Canadian couple who we met was delighted with their purchase of a large number of beautiful paintings with which they were going to furnish their newly purchased home in Canada. There is a lot of scenic beauty in Ubud, notable amongst it the sprawling paddy fields. In fact, there are identified viewing points that provide the best views of these fields.

The main attraction for tourist coming to Bali is in its beaches that have everything to offer and make the most popular destination with the tourists.

Caribbean Cruise – Nov' 2009

We went on a cruise to the Caribbean to celebrate our Ruby Wedding Anniversary. We flew into Miami to board our ship 'Ruby Princess' at Fort Lauderdale to an itinerary of Bahamas, St Kitts, Antigua, St Lucia and Barbados. As we had some time to spare, the driver of the coach decided to give us a guided tour of Miami. He took us to one particular area where the houses had roads in front and sea at the back for the rich residents to park their yachts on one side and have access to the city by car from the other side.

Cruise ships normally offer two options for dining. You can either go for 'seated dining' where you are allocated a table in one of the restaurants and your meals are served at the table, or you can go for 'buffet' service where you can go to any of the open restaurants and help yourself to the buffet style meal. We had chosen seated dining for this particular cruise. One thing I have always done on a cruise is to make contact with the Maitre d' or the restaurant manager to discuss our vegetarian meal requirements. Most of the ships have a number of Indian chefs amongst their staff and normally they would agree to provide us with Indian meals. They did the same on this cruise too and advised us to inform the waiter of our requirement for the following day in advance.

During the course of the first day, a lecture was held in the auditorium explaining about our cruise and various attractions that were available on the ports of call. There seemed to be great emphasis on the quality, variety and pricing of diamonds available on our first port of call, Bahamas. In the evening, we went to our table, which we were sharing with two other couples. One of them was a smart English couple from Kent with whom we became quite friendly and enjoyed our meal with them.

Next morning, our first port of call was Princess Kays in Bahamas. As we came out of the port, the very first thing we saw right in front was a huge diamond store. We decided to have a quick browse and Veena happened to like a necklace which I bought as a wedding anniversary gift for her. After a walk around the town, we wandered back to the ship in the evening.

I had ordered a bottle of champagne for dinner to celebrate our special day. The crew on the ship was aware of our wedding anniversary and they sent a cake along with the bottle of champagne to our table. We shared the bottle with our friends from Kent and finished the whole bottle. The couple was a developer and the husband narrated an incident about how cleverly he purchased two adjoining properties in an auction. He took one of his big burly African staff with him to the auction. When the first property came up for auction, my friend asked his chap to make the bids ensuring he is clearly visible while doing it. The first property went for competitive bidding with my friend winning it. But when the adjoining property came up for bidding, most people in the room knew who their resident neighbour was going to be and it sold at a much lower value. After dinner, we went to the casino and our friend insisted on buying us a drink there.

Next day a couple of Indian ladies, mother and daughter, approached us and introduced themselves. As they were travelling on their own, they asked if they could join us for company on excursions that we may be taking. They seemed pleasant enough and we did not see any objection to it. Our next port was St Kitts and the only thing of any interest listed there was a train journey to take you around the island. Seeing that there was nothing else to do, we decided to take a cab to the station to catch the train. But the cabby informed us that there was no ticket booth at the station and the only way to go on the train was to have booked the excursion in advance with the cruise operator. However, he offered us an alternative of taking us around by cab following more or less the same route and a bit extra. We accepted and were really pleased with his offer as we got so much more out of it. He took us around the island stopping at a number of places to let us enjoy the scenery and capture some good views.

At one point he stopped at a place where we could swing from the ropes like Tarzan. He climbed up on the side of the hill and intertwined some hanging vines together into a rope. Then he swung on it away from the hill and back. Hesitatingly, I had a go at it and quite enjoyed it inspiring the young girl to try it as well. As we were about to move from there, we noticed a group of people coming from one side. One of them had a huge cobra around his neck. He asked us to play with it if we wanted to and eventually, I ended up having the cobra around my neck.

Antigua was our next port of call. It is known to have so many beaches that you would not need to visit the same beach twice in a year. Then, we moved on to St Lucia, one of the most beautiful ports in the Caribbean and had a lovely sightseeing trip there. During the conversation, the two ladies accompanying us asked, "How come we don't see you at dinner time?" We told them that we had opted for seated dining and had Indian meals of our choice served to us every day. Rather amazed at this, they asked if they could join us one day. I told them to join us the following day but could not tell the waiter in advance. When I told the waiter that evening, he said, "Sir, don't worry! They can come anytime. We prepare enough quantity of your dishes and the surplus is enjoyed by the Indian staff in the kitchen later." The ladies joined us for dinner and were rather impressed with the treatment we were given.

Our final destination was Barbados with a unique experience of a ride in an Atlantis Submarine to explore the exquisite and colourful sea life and corals at the bottom of the sea. We were also taken to view the ruins of a ship that had sunk to the bottom of the sea near its coastline.

One thing I have not included above is the magnificent shows held every evening that are the hallmark of Princess and Caribbean cruises. There was another memorable event on the ship where they had set up a six feet high Christmas tree made up of champagne glasses. The Maitre d' went on top of the stage and started pouring champagne into the glass at the top of this tree. The champagne started trickling down to lower glasses giving a fountain-like effect filling the glasses from the top layers to the bottom. The Maitre d' started inviting the ladies from the audience to join him in pouring the champagne. He also asked Veena to join and I have a beautiful picture of her in a maroon red silk *saree* performing this.

Serene Europe – May 2009

We had never taken a conducted tour before but had heard a lot about Star Tours, in particular about their excellent vegetarian meals always delivered hot even in the middle of a journey. We decided to go on a Serene Europe tour with them, which was to cover Amsterdam, ZeeBrugge (Brussels) and Germany. The coach was to pick us up from Barking and Sasha dropped us off at the pick-up point. A few people were already there and they were all young couples. Some of them appeared to be on their honeymoon and some had little kids with them. As we boarded the coach, we observed the same pattern in the coach too. After a while, we started talking to each other and they realised that we mixed well with the whole group and they all started addressing us as uncle and aunty.

Our first stopover for sightseeing was Zeebrugge. There we realised that Thornton's and Lindt were not the best names in chocolates but it was Godiva, which has a price tag to match its reputation.

We visited Keukenhof Gardens in Amsterdam that is perhaps the best and the most scenic and colourful garden in the world. Everything is so well manicured that it feels as if not a blade of grass is out of place. It had a tremendous display of tulips, which were at their peak of bloom, and various other flowers. The layout of the garden with a lake with a fountain in the middle and weeping willow trees, added a beauty of its own. Although it had started raining, everyone was out taking pictures and videos.

Our coach journeys were filled with laughter and fun with singing of Bollywood songs, playing 'antakshari' and cracking jokes. As we were passing through the Dutch countryside, there were attractions on both sides with colourful fields of tulips, windmills and the like. The group devised a plan to make sure that no one missed any of these sights. People on the left of the coach would shout 'left' if there was something interesting on their side and the other side would similarly call 'right'. Everyone would turn to look at the side being called and it became such a fun journey.

We visited Frankfurt in Germany and were staying at a small hotel where probably we were the only group that evening. Their kitchen staff left and handed over the kitchen to Star Tours cooks who prepared a delicious Indian meal for us. We ended the trip feeling and behaving like 25-30 years old.

Barcelona – Jan' 2011

Barcelona is a city that is perhaps on every traveller's bucket list of 'to-visit'. Although I cannot point to a unique selling point but there is a kind of quirkiness and an atmosphere there that makes a visit to the city a pleasure. Beauty of Gaudi's design is everywhere to see. The colourful layout and design of Gaudi's Park Guell, the unique architecture and beauty of La Sagrada Familia church and La Casa, the last residence designed by Gaudi, is a treat for the senses. The buzz and atmosphere experienced during a walk down La Rambla (the Ramblas) or the beach leaves you with a sense of joy. A very large sculpture of a fish made in metal with lattice effect occupies a prominent position on the beach and is one of the best sculptures I have seen anywhere in the world. The sculpture is finished in rolled gold and provides a shimmering effect under sunlight.

Sasha had booked a very nice self-contained apartment right in the heart of the city within 5minutes walk from Catalonia Square. We would use every opportunity to just walk out and explore the various attractions. Another attraction very close to us was the Music Concert Hall (Palau de la Música Catalana) that was renowned for its ancient Catalonian architecture and magnificent stained glass work inside the main auditorium. The price difference between the tourist ticket for viewing the auditorium or to see a concert was not much. So, we decided to opt for the later.

The Rambla (La Rambla) was like the main shopping centre of any western city with shops, large department stores and grocery stores. It would always be full of shoppers and tourists. Catalonia Square at the end of it served as a nice meeting point for the people. One of the major roads running parallel to the Rambla was a much quieter tree-lined avenue, known locally as little Rambla. It was perfect for a nice stroll on a lazy sunny afternoon.

On one of our days there, a semi-final match was being played between India and Pakistan and I decided to watch it in a pub. There was a huge crowd of Pakistan supporters at the bar and a group of 5-6 youngsters supporting India at one end of the pub. I joined this group as both groups were shouting encouragement for their teams. India won the match and the nice thing was that Pakistan supporters came to our corner to congratulate us.

We were cautioned to be on guard against the pickpockets in Barcelona and did encounter one such incident. The three of us were waiting to catch the metro at the local station. As the train arrived, one burly gentleman and few others came between me, Veena and Sasha separating us. As I got pushed into the train, I started to look for Sasha and Veena but did not see them board after me. However, they kept their wits and quickly moved to the other entrance and entered the same compartment from there. To my utmost relief, I could soon see them waving to me from the other side. The burly chap kept trying to muscle in next to me while I was holding on to the pole in the middle of the compartment but I did not let him succeed. Soon I walked away from there to join Veena and Sasha.

One day, we decided to go for an Indian meal and were recommended a restaurant by the name of Govinda, which was not too far from our apartment. We entered the restaurant and were greeted by a gentleman sporting a ponytail like the Hare Krishna followers. Between its name and the manner in which the staff was dressed, we could guess that the restaurant was either owned by Hare Krishna movement or affiliated to it. It turned out to be a pure vegetarian restaurant and served a really nice meal to our taste.

We also took a guided tour of the city to enable us to see their Olympic Stadium, Picasso Museum, the stadium of FC Barcelona and the beaches. Barcelona will certainly remain on my bucket list of 'to visit again' places.

Bergen and Fjords of Norway Cruise – Jul' 2011

Cruise to the Norwegian Fjords was a totally different experience from any other cruise as it captured the scenic splendour of the fjords, the magnificent falls and the mountains surrounding the narrow waterways. We covered Stavanger, Eidfjord, Skjolden, Geiranger, Rosendal and Flam railway to Bergen.

Stavanger was the first port of call, which offered an insight into the Norwegian way of life. We took a tour of the city to experience its various attractions including the petrol museum and its agricultural landscape. At Eidfjord, we had an opportunity to visit the Hardanger glacier and the Hardangervidda national park that is the largest national park in Norway.

At Geiranger we took an excursion on a small inflatable boat into the Geirangerfjord. It is listed as one of nature's masterpieces and the most beautiful fjord on UNESCO's World Heritage site. It has some of the most majestic waterfalls like The Seven Sisters and is surrounded by the prettiest mountainous landscape. At one point, the guide pointed to a lonely cottage high up on the mountain and told us an interesting story about the old couple that lived there. They would primarily live off what they could grow in their farm and the animals that they kept. One day the husband of this lady had a blackout and she had to lug him over her shoulder to bring him all the way down to the bottom of the mountain to take a boat to the hospital. Fortunately, he recovered as they reached the bottom and the poor girl had to carry him all the way back up again. We also had an excursion on a kayak, which managed to take us behind one of the waterfalls.

The Flam railway journey to Bergen offered an opportunity to see some of the best sceneries covering the mountain valleys and cascading waterfalls. The variety and beauty of the waterfalls was simply admirable. There was one waterfall called 'The Veil' which covered the face of the mountain like a wedding veil.

Marrakesh – Sep' 2011

We decided to go on a short break to Marrakesh and found a very nice hotel named Albatros Garden. It had a charming interior of mosaic work, good food and excellent other facilities.

Marrakesh is not a modern country and a tour of the city turned out to be a rather simple affair. However, we did visit a gallery where they were making and displaying earthenware artefacts that were so fine that light could pass through them. Another interesting attraction was a visit to an evening show with lavish dinner. The show created a scene of war with chariots and was followed by a procession with a belly dancer on one of the chariots.

Cruise to Alaska_May 2012:

The experience of a cruise to Alaska is not something that you can describe in words. Activities like dog-sledding on top of a glacier, zip-ride on the longest zip-line, watching whales and sight of those massive ice-falls from the glaciers are some of the unique lifetime experiences that cannot be repeated elsewhere.

We had arranged this cruise with Sasha and my best mate from school days Vinod and his wife Gita. We planned a week's stay at Vancouver for a trip to the Canadian Rockies. However the timing did not work out for this to happen. Staying in an apartment just down the road from the famous Stanley Park, we spent an enjoyable time in Vancouver visiting Whistler, venue of winter Olympics, a visit to the Grouse Mountain and the suspension bridge and visiting the local attractions.

We boarded the Royal Caribbean's Radiance of the Seas from Canada Place. The size of the ship allowed it to come really close to the Hubbard glacier to enable us to observe parts of it break off like an ice-fall. Although the sight of this was amazing but it also reminded us of the disturbing effects of climate change.

At Icy Strait Point we had arranged the zip-line excursion. A little apprehensive initially, we arrived at the hilltop and noticed the warning about 'not suitable for people with heart condition'. I chose to ignore this and went ahead.

We were securely strapped in our bucket like seats and positioned just behind a horizontal bar. As the siren went, the bar lifted and our chair was thrown forward into the abyss. The feeling of being in a free fall for the first few seconds was only added to by the exhilaration of travelling on the line at speeds of over 60 mph.

The helicopter ride and dog sledding on the Mendenhall glacier is something one cannot forget about. From the helicopter the surface of the glacier appeared like a field of wheat crop. The ride with the sled being pulled by fierce huskies over this vast expanse of snow was truly amazing.

Finally at the end of our cruise we reached Seaward and boarded the train for a 4-hour journey to Anchorage. The scenery all along this journey was so magical and changing from moment to moment that you could just not take your eyes of the view.

Dubai – Sep' 2012

On our way to visit India to attend my niece Anubha's wedding, we decided to have a short break in Dubai and booked accommodation at the Savoy Suites Hotel Apartments.

We had heard of the luxury of Burj Al Arab (the only seven-star hotel in the world), Burj Khalifa, Atlantis the Palm and Jumeirah Zabeel Saray hotel. Besides visiting these, we were also keen to explore the malls and other shopping venues.

Burj Al Arab does not allow tourists to enter the premises without a reservation. So, we had made a reservation for High Tea in advance before we set off for Dubai. From the gate to the hotel, we took the buggy provided for the guests. As we set foot at the hotel entrance, we were welcomed by a spacious, high ceiling lobby with glittering gold paint and gold ornaments. We spent some time there taking it all in and of course took a lot of pictures. We made our way to the top floor of the hotel to the Skyview Bar for our High Tea. The bar itself is set up luxuriously in blue and provides a beautiful view of Palm Islands, the sea and a panoramic view of the city. We were seated at our table and served a glass of champagne and a selection of sandwiches. The tray for the sandwiches was also shaped like a sail replicating the profile of the hotel. Once we finished the first drink, we were served the tea along with sweet pastries, cakes and tarts. It was a delightful treat with a view to match. On the way back we took a slow stroll, admiring the scenario, the beach and the Persian Gulf.

The Burj Khalifa on the other hand has stunning observatories and a ticket for one of these gains you entry to the hotel. We chose the observatory 'At The Top' located on the 124th and 125th floors. Our experience began with a high-speed elevator ride to our floor that had a running commentary on the creation of the Burj Khalifa and the history of Dubai. It was late in the evening so we could see the vibrant cityscape and took our time to relax and enjoy exploring Dubai's architecture and history.

We came down from there to join hordes of people waiting around the square to watch the amazing display of water art, a grand symphony of music and dancing lights known as 'Dancing Fountain'. This is perhaps the most extravagant display of its kind in the world.

Our next day was aimed at Palm Jumeirah to visit The Atlantis and the Zabeel Saray hotels. The Atlantis again does not have an open-door policy for the tourists. So, I used the beachside entrance and pretended that my wife was inside and I had forgotten to bring my ID. When you say something with enough conviction not many people can dare to argue. And I managed to enter the Atlantis. Once I was inside, I went to the main entrance and invited Sasha and Veena in. The hotel's interior is a beautiful work of art with a tall unique coloured glass feature as a centrepiece. There is a beautifully laid out beach at the back with a large swimming pool. One special attraction at the hotel is an ATM machine that dispenses real gold in the form of coins, biscuits and bars. There is also a large aquarium with huge selection of fish and couple of people in wet suites doing an acrobatics display. There are a number of other activities organized by the hotel like a water park and some children's play areas. Sasha went for a swim with the dolphins in one of the activity areas. Again, a lot of photo opportunities.

We were awestruck as we entered the Zabeel Saray hotel, as the amount of gold paint and features on display is absolutely astounding. One thing that appealed to me is that it is all very artistically used to give the hall an elegant and luxurious feel. The hotel also has an amazing pool by the beach - an ideal place to relax with a drink.

The visit to the Dubai Mall, the largest mall in the world, was an experience to remember. There is hardly a famous brand name that did not have a presence there. Right in the middle of the hall as you enter the mall is an absolutely enormous aquarium. Following the visit to the mall, we went to the gold market, which has shops end to end, selling gold in all shapes and sizes. All that remained was a visit to the fake goods market where you can find copy of any famous brand. The shops have a queer arrangement with the display cabinets opening to rooms behind and leading to other hidden areas. I don't think we were keen to buy anything here and the visit was just to satisfy our curiosity.

Mystic Kerala– Sep' 2012

We reached Delhi to attend Anubha's wedding, which was a magnificent affair. Since we had some spare time after the wedding, we decided to take a trip to Kerala that had been on our bucket list for a long time. Along with Sasha who had gone with us, Dharam and Sunita had also come to attend the wedding and happily decided to join us for the trip. We contacted a travel agent in Delhi and asked him to make all the arrangements informing him of the places we were interested in visiting. The agent did a very good job of it booking the finest resorts and also arranged a seven-seater Innova car for us for the entire journey.

We drove from Cochin airport to see what is known as Indian Niagara Falls. But due to shortage of water, the place was not as we had hoped it to be and it turned to be a simple waterfall. Driving on to Munnar we stayed at ITDC's Tea County Resort that had lovely sloping gardens at the back leading onto the sandy beach. The visit to Kannan Devan Tea Museum showed us the whole process of making tea and the varieties of it. I have certainly acquired a taste for their Premium Green tea that I brought from there with me.

Beauty of Kerala lies in its lush greenery enhanced by the undulating landscape of tea plantations and in its serene backwaters with the surrounding scenery. We got plenty of evidence of the former in our travel to the National Park and the Dam.

We moved on from Munnar to Kumarakom where we stayed at the newly built Hotel Vasundhara Sarovar Premier. We took a boat from the backwaters just behind the hotel for a sunset cruise in the evening. After our dinner at the hotel, we enjoyed the enchanting programme of music that had been arranged at the hotel. Next morning, we drove to Aleppey to board a houseboat for our trip on the backwaters. The boat had been stocked with food and we added our own drinks to it. It felt so serene cruising at a gentle pace in the still waters with sights of fishing nets, people living around backwaters going about their activity, palm trees swaying in gentle breeze and other houseboats. We travelled for a few hours enjoying the views and then moored at a point for the rest of the night. The cook on the boat prepared the food and we enjoyed it thoroughly with our drinks. We got into the mood for singing and played some games and had a good laugh.

Next morning the driver picked us up to take us to our hotel Samudra Beach Resort in Kovalam. After breakfast we made our way to the Vivekananda Rock Memorial, on a small island off the coast of Kanyakumari. It is also referred to as 'Land's End' and you can see the merging (confluence) of Indian Ocean, Bay of Bengal and Arabian Sea at its tip. Our final destination was the Padmanabhaswami temple with its magnificent structure. The temple has gained popularity recently for the contents of its vaults, which are believed to be worth billions of dollars.

Baltics Cruise – Jun' 2013

Our Baltics Cruise covered places like Southampton, Oslo, Copenhagen, Stockholm, Helsinki, St Petersburg and Tallinn. The first port of call was Oslo the capital of

Norway, a country that is famous for its fjords surrounded by hills and forests. The Scandinavian countries' reputation of a permissive society was well in evidence on our visit to the Vigaland Sculpture Park. The Park is a result of the artist's obsession and a lifetime of work dedicated to the human form which took him over 20 years to complete. It contains 212 bronze and granite sculptures showing naked human bodies in various endeavours in single or group formations.

The visit to statue of little mermaid in Copenhagen turned out to be a damp squib due to it being a very small statue and not much else to see around there. Tivoli gardens amusement park was a mixture of buildings in exotic styles, theatre, bandstands, restaurants, cafes, flower gardens and rides. There were a number of attractions that made it a popular tourist attraction for the whole family.

Stockholm, our next port of call is the cultural, media, political and economic centre of Sweden. It is a fast-changing metropolis abuzz with design, fashion, innovation and technology. There was not much of interest for us to see in the city.

Helsinki, the capital of Finland, is a relatively young city and can be seen as a melting pot of eastern and western Europe. It has some of the best neoclassical architecture and a large number of parks that make it very attractive in summer.

St Petersburg, the cultural capital of Russia is renowned for its unique golden spires, gilded domes, cathedrals, museums and palaces. The palaces are reminiscent of it having been the USSR's imperial capital for two centuries. As soon as you enter the Catherine's Palace you are awe stuck by the sheer opulence of its gilded interior with exquisite architecture, décor and artefacts. The Peterhof Palace and gardens is equally impressive in its exterior and interior glamour. The huge gardens have some exquisite water features and one of the best fountain displays. The gilded artefacts and figurines do not just limit to the palace but also find a place around the fountain in the form of animals, mermaids and humans. We have seen many palaces in England and the Palace of Versailles too but these two were really something else. Other places that we visited were the Hermitage Museum with its display of some beautiful artefacts, amongst them the oldest moving and talking cuckoo clock, the Church of the Savior on Spilled Blood and Palace Square, popular with the newlyweds to visit.

Mediterranean Cruise - May 2014

This was a cruise we took with our kitty group and it turned out to be a thoroughly enjoyable trip with a lot of fun and laughter. We had been to the Mediterranean before but were happy to do another trip with a slightly different itinerary. We boarded the P&O Cruise ship Aurora from Southampton calling at St Peter Port Guernsey, La Rochelle France, Bilbao in Spain and Ferrol in Spain before returning to Southampton.

The ship had some of the best facilities including sports activities, swimming, gym, jogging track on the deck and entertaining evening shows. One of the attractions was a 'ball tracking golf driving range'. They held a competition in the range to hit the ball closest to the pin. Being a novice golfer, I decided to have a go at it and fluked into second position.

With 11 members in our group there was never a shortage of activities or company. We enjoyed playing table tennis, some of us would go to the gym while others went for morning walks on the track. But maximum fun was in the evenings playing cards, enjoying a few drinks and having a general chitchat. The outings at the ports of call were enjoyable and gave us an opportunity to sample the history and culture of the places.

The British Isle of Guernsey is a fishing port and is the oldest settlement in Channel Islands. Its cobbled streets and granite houses make a spectacular backdrop to the magnificent harbour.

La Rochelle, another fishing port is an attractive resort boasting of fortified towers and 16th century mansions. Colourful yachts and pavement cafes add to its charm and create a beautiful coastline. There is plenty to see in the town, along the coast and in the countryside.

Bilbao is the industrial and financial capital of the Basque country and is situated between two ranges of hills on both sides of river Nervion. One of the prime attractions is the famous Guggenheim Museum with its paintings and other contemporary works of art including one by Arcelor Mittal in steel.

Ferrol, in addition to being a fishing port was also a naval base. It was also home to some interesting naval museums and beautiful Santiago Cathedral.

Tunisia – Aug' 2014

We planned the trip to Tunisia with good friends of ours Beena and KG Khandelwal. The hotel in which we stayed was very nice and had good facilities including a large outdoor swimming pool and a semi-circular indoor swimming pool with glass ceiling and glass windows all round. However, it would appear that it was primarily a meat-eating country and apart from salads and fruits there was not much of a selection in vegetarian meals. Anyway, after a discussion with the restaurant manager, a vegetarian meal was prepared for us every day. Although I would not describe it as a delicious meal by any stretch of the imagination. On one occasion we were served rice and *daal* and asked the waiter to get us some spoons as they had kept only knives and forks on the table. He went away and never came back. KG called another waiter, pulled out his wodge of notes and slipped him a £20 note asking him to get us some spoons. The waiter went away and appeared after some time with four spoons.

KG had a peculiar habit that he never used a credit card or cheque but carried a bundle of notes with him. As we went for a meal at the airport, he decided to pay for it and took out his wallet full of notes. Realising that he may have smaller denominations, he took out his wodge of notes and gave a twenty-pound note from it. Beena was concerned that he could easily be a target of pickpockets and requested me to take care of all payments and that we could settle later.

There was not much to do or see in Tunisia apart from the amphitheatre and port and we had a very relaxing holiday.

Rhodes with the Family – Jun' 2015

This was a family holiday that all of us would remember with fond memories as it gave us quality time to spend with the family and in particular with Akaash, my grandson. We had booked an all-inclusive package at the Princess Andriana resort. It is a beautiful resort with a large swimming pool and all kinds of entertainment. There was specific entertainment laid on for kids that made it so much better for us as Akaash could be kept busy for a while if we wanted to do something else. The buffet restaurant is worth a mention as it serves the best selection and quality of vegetarian meals that I have eaten outside India. The selection of British desserts in the menu is also worth a mention.

As others did not fancy going to Prasonisi, I decided to go there on my own. It is a very small island connected to the main island by a very long but narrow strip of land. At low tide the land is visible and you can walk on it to reach the island. As the level of water rises, the land gets covered and creates an impression of you walking on water. The kite beach there is a popular destination for windsurfing and kite boarding.

Rhodes is the largest of Greece's island and at one time it was known to be the haunt of the rich and the famous. This is evident from the number of large yachts moored at the port. We made a day trip to the town visiting the Acropolis and the historic ruins, its medieval streets and the beach.

Cape Verdi with Sasha – Nov' 2015

For the next holiday we wanted to find a spot away from the popular touristy destinations. Sasha found a place called Cape Verde, an island off the coast of Africa, which was fast becoming a hot spot in this category. We booked an all-inclusive holiday in a lovely resort called Melia

Tortuga. The resort was on a beautiful clean sandy beach with a gentle sea, which made for a wonderful morning walk for us. Sometimes when you are at peace with yourself, you observe the beauty of nature intently. I remember experiencing one such incident during our morning walk. I saw a small bird sitting at the end of the beach. As the water of the sea would recede, it would gently follow its edge to catch the worms and as the waves turned outwards, it would make a dash for the shore trying to escape the rushing water. I remember staying there for quite some time enjoying this fascinating activity of the little bird.

The resort was set up like a small community village in England, with tree-lined avenues and cottages on both sides of the road. We had one of the cottages with a private pool of its own. All other facilities were available within the resort like a large swimming pool, a restaurant that served delicious selection of vegetarian meals, games room and a programme of variety entertainment every evening after dinner. There was another resort close by which also offered additional activities like massage and others.

The evening programme on the first day was 'Dances of Cape Verde', a dance based on African culture. The fast tempo and rhythm of the dance left everyone feeling exhilarated and wanting to join in. They had a session afterwards in which the dancers did simple steps which members from the audience could copy and enjoy. Next day we went to see the town centre. The main attraction there was a bar-cum-restaurant that was overhanging the sea and provided a beautiful view of the sea with people parasailing and doing other activities. The evening's entertainment programme on the second day was a musical event. Another evening they had a display of Capoeira, which is African-Brazilian martial art combining the elements of dance, acrobatics and music. This was followed on another evening by a colourful display of acrobatics and juggling. Overall, it was a very entertaining and relaxing holiday.

Historic Scotland – Sept' 2016

After our amazing Serene Europe experience with Star Tours, we decided to book the Historic Scotland excursion with them during my brother-in-law's visit to the UK. Our first visit was a coach trip to Nevis Range to savour the scenic beauty of the mountain. We spent the next day with a sightseeing tour of Glasgow city including the main square, University of Glasgow and Glasgow Cathedral capturing a lot of Scotland's culture and history. A similar tour of Edinburgh covered the city, Royal Mile and Edinburgh Castle.

We also visited the Neptune's Staircase that is a series of nine 'locks' on the Caledonian Canal covering a short length of 450 meters. When the canal goes through a steep slope in the landscape, the speed of the boat needs to be slowed by building a lock (dam) to arrest the flow of water. It consists of two sets of gates, one of which opens to allow the boat into a holding area. When the water in the holding area rises, the second gate opens to allow the water to recede and for the boat to exit at a lower level through the second gate. The tourist attraction of Neptune's Staircase is nine such gates in a quick succession that allow the water level to drop by nearly 20 metres. If you were to look at the series of locks from the bridge on the canal, it would appear like a staircase hence the name.

In an area nearby was another British invention known as Falkirk Wheel, which replicated the process of the lock by use of a large wheel. The boat would enter the wheel from one side of the canal, the wheel would turn by 180 degrees to lower the boat to the level of water on the other side and the boat would exit. It was a lucky coincidence that The Kelpies had been put on display in a park nearby. These are very large beautiful sculptures of two 'horse heads' in aluminium latticework, which glisten under sunlight.

A visit to Scottish highland would not be complete without a visit to a distillery. We were taken to visit Auchentoshan distillery in the west of Scotland, the name meaning 'corner of the field' in Celtic. This is the only distillery in the world that makes single malt whiskey that has been distilled three times (all other do this twice only).

A stopover in Lake District and a boat ride on the lake Windermere made the trip truly perfect.

Cyprus (Paphos) with Maneesh – May 2017

This was our second holiday with Maneesh's family and we all looked forward to being with Akaash. It certainly turned out to be a very lively and fun-filled holiday. We stayed at a resort named Avanti hotel. It had a bright and modern environment, excellent range of facilities including a large and decorative swimming pool, a beach in the vicinity and a number of dining options. Also included were a range of facilities for children like an activity playground, children's club with various activities and some arranged programmes in the evenings. We thoroughly enjoyed the quality time spent with Akaash there.

Kos with Sasha – Oct' 2017

This holiday has left us with some mixed memories. I had booked a couple of holidays before using recommendation from a travel advisory website Secret Escapes and booked this very nice-looking resort in Kos. We had booked two adjoining rooms for Sasha and us. When we arrived at the hotel, Sasha did not like the smell in her room and was not willing to stay in it. The manager changed her room but she had to be in a different area from us. Although the hotel generally had good facilities but the vegetarian meal selection was rather limited and left a lot to be desired. Somehow, we managed to get this sorted and could have decent meals. Thankfully the hotel had a nice pool and some entertainment.

There are plenty of long sandy beaches in Kos with water warm enough to swim in the sea. The town and harbour are one of the attractions. We took an excursion to one of the small islands, which had a population in double figures only. Yet the place was very well kept with a lot of eating places and a lovely sandy beach. We wondered why they needed so many eating-places for the size of the population. We figured that perhaps this was their main source of income during tourist season and they had to live off that earning for the rest of the year.

Electrifying Japan – May 2018:

I have always had respect and admiration for Japan for its national character and its excellence in technological advancement. The country was totally decimated after world war two but the way its leadership focused on building a spirit of nationalism and move forward, forgiving the enemy, has enabled it to rise to become one of the top economies again. Pride in their work forms a part of their national character and failure to deliver results has a stigma attached to it that unfortunately results in a high rate of suicide amongst Japanese people. This pride and discipline reflected in all the places looking spic and span and everything working like clockwork. The bullet trains arrived at the stations on the dot of time and departed precisely 90 seconds later.

Ours was an organised group tour with 26 of friends and 'friends of friends' in the group. We had a tour guide accompanying us all the way from UK and another Japanese guide who took us around the places in Japan joined him.

The tour itinerary covered Tokyo, Hakone, Nagoya, bullet train to Hiroshima, bullet train to Kyoto and Osaka.

Buddhist temples and Shinto shrines form a significant part of Japanese history and culture. In addition, the amazing colours and traditional design of these makes them a must for any tourist's itinerary. Shinto is the oldest religion that originated in Japan. Buddhism, as we know originated in India as a contemporary of Jainism, and spread to many countries including Japan. Shinto shrines have a symbolic entrance known as Torii gate, which is made of two pillars with an arched bar on the top. One of the most publicised and well known of these is the Fushimi Inari shrine in Kyoto that has thousands of torii gates.

Itsukushima shrine located on the island of Miyajima, just outside Hiroshima, is built on stilts over the sea with its red 'torii gate', which looks as if it's floating on water. The site is listed as a UNESCO World Heritage Site. The shrine is not only full of rich culture and history; it's also an incredibly beautiful place to walk around, particularly at night, when the shrine is fully lit up.

Our itinerary also included a number of temples namely Senso-ji, the oldest and one of the most impressive temples in Tokyo, Kotokuin temple in Yokohoma with the second largest statue of Buddha made in Bronze, Kinakuji temple in Kyoto and the Todai-ji temple in the Nara Deer Park in Osaka.

In Tokyo, we visited the beautiful Shinjuku Gyoen gardens and Nakamese shopping arcade and were amazed to see the Japanese national character first hand. A young man in a smart suit was walking towards us. Suddenly, we saw him bend down and kneel to pick up something from the floor. On coming close, we realised that he had spotted a chewing gum stuck to the floor and was removing it with his nails.

After lunch we went to see the Imperial Palace from outside. In Yokohama, sister city to Mumbai, we visited the Yamashita Park and amongst the beautiful display of flowers we also saw the Water Fountain that had been donated to the town by the Indians.

Our guide took us for an exclusive Japanese meal to find that it was a DIY (do it yourself) affair. We were seated at tables for four, two on each side with a large 4-piece hotplate in the middle of the table. The waiters delivered noodles, chopped salad and various sauces and spices and left. We were to make our own noodles using whatever recipe we fancied. It turned to be good fun and quite an affair as we were all trying different things and sharing later to compare who had mastered the art.

From Hakone we drove by coach to the 5th station for some beautiful views of Mt Fuji and then onwards to the Picasso Museum with it's enchanting 'mobile' and 'still' sculptures. This was followed by a visit to Toyota Museum in Nagoya. An exciting Bullet train journey from Nagoya took us to Hiroshima. When we hear about the millions of people who died from the atomic bomb in Hiroshima it does not have quite the same impact as does a visit to the Peace Memorial Museum. The pictorial demonstration of the dropping of the atom bomb and resulting destruction was so horrific that we all had tears in our eyes. I had to sit down to meditate for 10 minutes before I could come out of the building.

We then took a bullet train from Hiroshima to Kyoto, visited the temple and watched a Kimono show. Then we proceeded to Osaka for a visit to the castle, the temple and Dotonbori market. We went to an Indian restaurant for the evening meal. They had very good music playing and our group was quick to take to the floor and have an enjoyable evening of song and dance.

The best part of the whole trip was the company, as we would sing songs, crack jokes and have lots of fun. There were also plenty of Indian sweets and savouries being passed around during all the coach journeys. A very pleasant trip indeed would be the verdict!

Rajasthan and Gujarat – Dec' 2018

We were sitting at home one day discussing our next holiday. Veena suggested a trip to India covering Rajasthan and Gujarat adding that there was a lot to see in India and we had not really seen much of it. Although I had been to Rajasthan earlier, but thought it would be good to visit it again together as a family. I started working on the places that we could include in our trip. Some notable ones that sprang to mind were Jaipur, Udaipur, Ranakpur and Mt. Abu in Rajasthan and Rann of Kutch, Ahmedabad and Gir Forest in Gujarat. Veena wanted to go to Somnath and Dwarka also in Gujarat, and Mahadev's temple in Pushkar, which was going to fall on our way as informed by one of her friends. As we were to go past Agra, we decided to include a visit to Taj Mahal also. A friend of mine from Gujarat suggested that if we were visiting Gujarat, we could not afford to miss the temple in Palitana. Looking at the way our itinerary was developing, I told Veena that it was becoming more like a pilgrimage (tirth-yatra) rather than a holiday. But we were both happy with our selection. Although Ranakpur and Mt. Abu are places of historic interest to all tourists but it has several Jain temples too which are worth a visit.

I booked an air-conditioned Toyota Innova, a seven-seater SUV for the entire journey and was going to start booking the hotels in Rajasthan. This is when one of our friends mentioned about their family who was in travel business and could perhaps make all the necessary arrangements for us. I spoke to the travel organisers who took care of all the arrangements for us from here on. They booked hotels, visits to places of interest including the Gir forest safari and guides at different places. The car hire firm was based in Ahmedabad but agreed to have the car sent to us in Delhi.

When we discussed our itinerary with our nephew in Delhi, he expressed concern about it being a rather straining journey for our age and suggested that if we felt tired at any point we should come straight back. The very first hotel at Agra was an excellent one with views of the Taj Mahal directly from our bedroom window. We spent a couple of days at Agra and moved on to Shiv Vilas Resort in Jaipur, which is a 'palace theme' resort. It was a delightful place and as we got off the car there were musicians playing *shehnai* and flute at the entrance. As we entered the lobby, we had to walk through rows of staff lined up with folded hands. Then we were garlanded and a *tilak* was put on our foreheads. The place was as magnificent from inside as it was from outside. We stayed there for two days visiting all the attractions. Our driver was superbly knowledgeable about all the routes and places of interest throughout Rajasthan and Gujarat and showed all of them with little time wasted. We also happened to visit a carpet factory and saw the whole process of making a carpet by hand. We were amazed at the selection of carpets they had varying from all wool, cashmere and silk and wool mix carpets. We finally decided to buy a carpet for our sitting room there and then.

Next morning, we left for Pushkar, stayed overnight at Ajmer and went to visit the temple. Our next stop was Udaipur where we stayed at Gulab Nivas, which was a delightful *haveli* style hotel on the bank of Lake Pichola with a clear view of Taj Lake Palace. The meals at our hotel were excellent with music playing during the dinners. We visited all the main attractions of the city including the City Palace and the Lake Palace Gardens.

We drove next to Ranakpur to see the historic and most iconic architectural Jain temple. The beauty of the temple from any angle from outside as well inside is awe-inspiring. The temple has 1444 sculpted marble pillars where no two pillars are the same. The rest of the architecture in the temple is equally magnificent and it represents perhaps one of the best architectures in India.

Our next stop was Mt. Abu and a visit to another Jain temple of parallel beauty as the Ranakpur temple. The hotel we stayed in was a small family-run hotel with good Rajasthani food. They had set up a program in the front lawn of the hotel in the evening. As it was a cold night, they had put some fires so that we could around it and enjoy the folk music of Rajasthan followed by some Bollywood music.

From Mt. Abu, we drove to Rann of Kutch and stayed at the Tent City. It was one of our longest continuous journeys and we reached there late at night. The tents were of good quality with all modern amenities built inside them. We went to the Rann early next morning to view the sunrise. The first view of the Rann with flat white salt stretched out to miles was a sight to behold. It was further enhanced by the rising sun. The food at the Tent City was a huge selection of all Rajasthani dishes and we were really spoiled for choice. There was entertainment arranged for the evenings and a fair number of activities during the daytime. We visited the black mountain in the evening to view the sunset, which was again a sight to behold.

Our next stop was Ahmedabad where we were hoping to have a day of rest. However, our driver being a local boy insisted that we go to see the newly built Statue of Unity. It is a truly inspiring structure of Sardar Patel. Although the infrastructure had all been nicely built, it was 'work in progress' in developing the surrounding area.

Our next stop was Palitana and we made an early start from our hotel to the hills where the temple structures are situated. It is not just one temple but a range of temples spread over a large area. Architectural beauty of each temple is equally magnificent.

Next morning, we went to Sasan Gir forest where our accommodation had been arranged at the Gir Lion Safari camp. We had an early morning start for the safari and our driver asked us to leave the hotel by 5:30 am. The safari was ready for us when we reached there and we were put on an open top jeep. We found it a bit surprising to see that neither the driver nor the guide with him were armed in any way. The guide informed us that not every safari may get an opportunity to see the lion. In fact, sometimes visitors had come for a safari for three days in a row and never saw a single lion. However, he also mentioned that the lions normally went to drink water in the morning, which was the best time for viewing them. We went on our route and after a while saw a group of jeeps assembled in one place and stopped there. Finally, we caught the sight of a majestic lion on one side of the forest. As we carried on further, we also spotted a black jaguar.

After a satisfied safari, the same day we drove to the hotel in Somnath and visited the temple the next day. Somnath temple has been rebuilt into an impressive structure and has a light and sound show on the temple in the evening. Next morning, we went on the last leg of our journey to Dwarka and visited the *bhet*-Dwarka temple and the main

Dwarka temple. We finally took a flight back to Delhi from Rajkot airport.

The successful journey was topped by an icing on the cake by two celebrations of our upcoming golden wedding anniversary in Gurgaon and Delhi.

Mediterranean Cruise with Family – October 2019

To celebrate our golden wedding anniversary, our children decided to treat us to a family holiday with a cruise to the Mediterranean. They booked a lovely suite with a balcony for us on Norwegian Star. We boarded the ship at Venice and travelled to Montenegro, Corfu, Santorini (Greece), Argostoli (Kefalonia) and Dubrovnik. It was a lovely holiday that gave us an opportunity to spend time together as a family, explore various locations enroute and enjoy the entertainment and facilities on the ship.

Goa and 50th Anniversary in Delhi – Jan' 2020

We had just celebrated our golden wedding anniversary and I wanted to give Veena a real treat. I felt that a long-awaited trip to Goa would perfectly fit the bill. I started by looking at the five-star hotels and resorts in Goa and after reading the customer's reviews and checking the facilities on offer, decided to book a suite at The Lalit Spa and Golf resort.

The resort is spread over an area of over 100 acres, has its own private beach and a 9-hole golf course, perhaps the only one in Goa. Other facilities include a gym, massage, spa, sauna and a sports area with tennis, badminton, squash courts and a games area with table tennis, carrom board and cards. Our suite, facing the swimming pool, was quite large with all the modern amenities one would expect in a five-star hotel. The variety and quality of food was absolutely top notch and I used to specially look out for the evening buffet with a touch of North and South Indian as well as European dishes. Very soon we formed a daily routine that started with a walk along the golden sandy beach followed by Veena having her massage at one of the beach huts. Following breakfast, we would walk down or take golf buggy to the sports area and spend some time playing table tennis, carrom and some card games. Sometime in the day, I would also try to catch a swim in the pool. I also managed to play a few rounds of golf during our stay.

We made a sightseeing trip to the town to view the church and some popular beaches like Dona Paula, Anjuna and Candolim. Our friends Ajay and Saroj Aggarwal came to visit us for a day and were very impressed with the resort. They agreed to come together with us to stay there next time. We took them out to Candolim beach for a meal at a popular beachside restaurant watching the sunset.

A very pleasant and relaxing holiday.

With my interest in photography, I have captured the photos and videos that we have taken during all our holidays and converted them into videos on YouTube.

8. Retirement and Beyond

PREPARED FOR RETIREMENT

As it was coming close to the time of retirement, I started to think about planning for the same. Two questions that come into everyone's mind at a time like this is about finances and about all the time that you will have at your disposal.

It was surprising that finances were not a problem at all and we could maintain the same lifestyle and standard of living without any change.

To make the best use of time, I decided to learn some new skills and took lessons in bridge, golf and also joined the gym to learn to swim. This enabled me to join a couple of bridge clubs and also enjoy a game of golf a couple of times a week.

I was already actively involved in the Jain Association and was elected as President soon after my retirement.

Voluntary and Community Service:

I decided to take up some other voluntary and community activities:

- Metropolitan Housing – I joined the board of Metropolitan Housing, one of the largest Housing Cooperatives in the UK, as a non-executive director. My role of Head of IT at Ascham Homes provided a useful background to this.

- Metropolitan Police Community Assessor – this turned out to be a very interesting role in the recruitment of detectives and officers in the police force in London.

- PPG and PEF – surgeries in UK run a Patient Participation Group to involve the patients in the provision of an effective service to its users. As it's vice chair I also became involved in the next level up, the Patient Engagement Forum which would provide the interface to the regional Clinical Commissioning Group of the National Health Service.

- Samarpan Music Group – the Hindu Cultural Society (HCS) in North London ran a music class under the guidance of a young and energetic teacher Arpan Patel. I decided to join this group and found it a very pleasant and enlightening experience. It also gave us the opportunity to give presentations at the functions held at the HCS and also at the celebration of India's Independence Day at Gymkhana Club. We also enjoyed various outings like dinners and attending musical events.

Development of Pyramid Puzzle App:

Some years ago I had purchased a puzzle at Christmas time and we had hours of fun playing with this at home. The logic and intricacy of this puzzle had fascinated me. I decided to enhance that puzzle and develop it into an IOS app for Apple devices.

I designed the whole thing around a tetrahedron with nine tiles on each face of the triangular pyramid. Each of these tiles had a pattern on its edge and the objective of the game was to place all the 36 tiles on the faces of the pyramid in such a way that the pattern on the edge of each tile would match the pattern on all its adjoining tiles.

I had the App finally developed in India and had it loaded on iTunes store in 2014. The puzzle had reasonable success and received good comments from the users. However, due to it being limited to IOS it did not have a wide reach. I am considering having the same developed for all three platforms – IOS, Android and Windows.

Publishing Book on Yoga:

With time on my hands I started practising yoga every morning. After attending Swami Ramdev's camp in 2006, I had already incorporated a number of *pranayams* in my routine. I also wanted to include meditation into the practice to see the additional benefits it may deliver. Using the principle of 'yoga nidra' I would start the practice with 'focussed breathing' with 'visualisation'. This way, making use of the full yoga breath, I would in turn relax the muscles in each leg and then move on to the arms, the lower back, upper back, neck and shoulders, head, face, abdomen and the chest. I found this 3-5 minute routine will take me in a near state of meditation and allow me to connect with my body and maintain a constant communication with the body while doing my practice.

Another consideration I had in mind was to keep the *asanas* simple yet effective for the whole body, to make it possible for a person of any age or ability to be able to perform these in the comfort of their own home and without any supervision.

The holistic approach of the practice made me feel so calm and peaceful at the end of the session that I called the practice 'Meditational Yoga' and produced the book as covered above.

Following this I developed a morning routine that would consist of daily cleansing (which would also cover neti every now and then) followed by yoga for an hour and a half, a cup of tea and catching up on news on TV, bath, prayer and breakfast. This four hour routine sets me up nicely for the day with a positive outlook,

The recent pandemic of Covid changed the lifestyle tremendously. This period of quiet made me look back at my life and the experience of writing the book on yoga and that is how I embarked on writing this book.

Printed in Great Britain
by Amazon